John and Sally McKenna's 'Bridgestone 100 Best' Guides give all the information you need to enjoy the best of Ireland. These places to stay are chosen for their comfort and hospitality, their individuality and their value for money, each earning the right to call themselves one of the 100 Best.

The Bridgestone 100 Best Guides to Ireland are the most up-to-the-minute annual guides you can buy. Intensively and dedicatedly researched, with a wealth of detail and description of the chosen entries and written with humour and personal experience, these are the essential travelling companions. If you wish to find the very best of Ireland, you need to travel with John and Sally McKenna's Bridgestone Guides.

Readers' praise for the Bridgestone Guides:

'Informative, extremely well written and, above all, accurate . . . I just wish there was something similar for England, Wales and Scotland'.
Mr. D.P., Thaxted, Essex.

'An excellent, entertaining and necessary guide to anyone hoping to find good food in this country'.
Mr. J. K., Crawley, Sussex.

'Your guidebook is a really good one because it does not mislead the reader but offers true and good advice. All the places we tried were all that your guide promised'.
Dr. C. B., Malta

'Without your knowledge and book we should not have had such a glorious holiday'.
Mrs. B. M., Athy, Co Kildare

First published in 1994 by
Estragon Press Ltd, Durrus, Bantry, Co Cork
© Estragon Press

Text © John McKenna and Sally McKenna 1994
Illustrations © Ken Buggy 1994
Maps © Ken Buggy 1994
Cover photo © Lucy Johnston 1994

The moral right of the authors has been asserted

ISBN 1 874076 09 X

Printed by Colour Books Ltd, Baldoyle, Co Dublin Tel: (01) 832 5812
Designed by Karl Tsigdinos/Gold Star Media, Dublin Tel: (01) 260 0899
Typeset by Seton Music Graphics, Bantry, Co. Cork Tel: (027) 50742
Cover Photo by Lucy Johnston, Garville Lane Studios Tel: (01) 496 0584

Cover photo taken at Avondale House, Castleknock, Dublin.

THE BRIDGESTONE
100 BEST PLACES TO STAY
IN IRELAND 1994

JOHN MCKENNA

SALLY MCKENNA

With illustrations by Ken Buggy

ESTRAGON PRESS

For Mary and Des

With thanks to:

Des Collins, Colm Conyngham, Karl, Lucy, Eddie, Elaine, Sarah Bates, Cynthia Harrison, Cathleen Buggy, Ray Buckley and John Harold, James O'Shea, Tom Owens, Robin Gourlay, Roger Lascelles, Ethna McKiernan, and Pat Ruane

John McKenna was born in Belfast and educated both there and in Dublin, where he practised as a barrister before turning to writing in 1989. His work appears in newspapers and magazines in Ireland and the U.K. In 1993 he won the Glenfiddich Regional Writer of the Year Award for journalism.

Sally McKenna was born in Kenya, and brought up on the Pacific island of Fiji before coming to Ireland in 1982. She cooked professionally before turning to writing about food and restaurants. She is a member of the accreditation panel of the Bio-dynamic Agricultural Association in Ireland.

Ken Buggy was born in Dublin in 1947 and has spent most of his working life abroad. He now lives in Kinsale with his wife Cathleen and their four children.

JOHN McKENNA and SALLY McKENNA won the first André Simon Special Commendation Award in 1992 for the second edition of The Bridgestone Irish Food Guide.

ULSTER

NORTH
CHAN

ATLANTIC OCEAN

BE

LONDONDERRY

ANTRIM

DONEGAL

TYRONE

DOWN

FERMANAGH

ARMAGH

SLIGO

MONAGHAN

CONNACHT

MAYO

LETTRIM

CAVAN

LOUTH

ROSCOMMON

LONGFORD

MEATH

WESTMEATH

GALWAY

OFFALY

KILDARE

DUBLIN

DUBLIN

LEINS

GALWAY

LAOIS

WICKLOW

IRIS
SE

N

W   E

S

CLARE

CARLOW

KILKENNY

TIPPERARY

LIMERICK

WEXFORD

WATERFORD

KERRY

CORK

MAP SHOWS COUNTY DIVISIONS
AND PROVENCES.

CORK

0   40   80 KMS

MUNSTER

0   15   50 MLS

BRIDGESTONE

Contents

BRIDGESTONE

BRIDGESTONE IS JAPAN'S LARGEST tyre manufacturer and one of the top three in the world. Founded in 1931, the company has striven to maintain an emphasis on technological advancement and service while expanding the scale and scope of its operations. As a result the company is recognised as a leader in tyre manufacturing and technology.

Bridgestone tyres are presently sold in more than 150 countries. There are twelve manufacturing plants in Japan with others throughout the world including the U.S.A. and Australia. Bridgestone now also manufactures its tyres in Europe following the acquisition in 1988 of the Firestone Tyre and Rubber Company.

They manufacture tyres for many different vehicles, from trucks and buses to passenger cars and motor-cycles. Its commercial vehicle tyres enjoy a worldwide reputation for superior cost-per-kilometre performance, and its aircraft tyres are used by more than 100 international airlines. Many Japanese cars imported to Ireland arrive with Bridgestone tyres and a host of exotic sports cars including Ferrari, Lamborghini, Porsche, Jaguar and TVR are now fitted with Bridgestone tyres as original equipment.

Bridgestone is at the forefront of tyre research and development. Its proving ground in Kuroiso City, Japan covers 400,000 square metres and consists of a 3.5 kilometre banked test track and skid pan which together contain more than 40 different road surfaces. Bridgestone also operate an advanced R&D facility in Kodaira, Japan. Testing focuses on a wide range of features including directional stability, skid resistance, durability, abrasion resistance, riding comfort and noise reduction. All this data is then put to valuable use in the development of new and better tyres. Bridgestone is now the most technologically advanced tyre manufacturer in the world.

In June 1990 Bridgestone (Ireland) Ltd was established as a subsidiary of the multinational Bridgestone Corporation to take over the distribution of its tyres in Ireland. The company operates from its offices and warehouse in Tallaght in Dublin where it stocks a wide range of passenger car, commercial vehicle and earthmover tyres. Bridgestone staff also provide sales, technical and delivery services all over the country.

● *Bridgestone tyres are available from tyre dealers throughout Ireland. For further information contact Bridgestone (Ireland) Ltd., Unit A30, Greenhills Industrial Estate, Tallaght, Dublin 24. Tel: (01) 452 7766 Fax: (01) 452 7478*

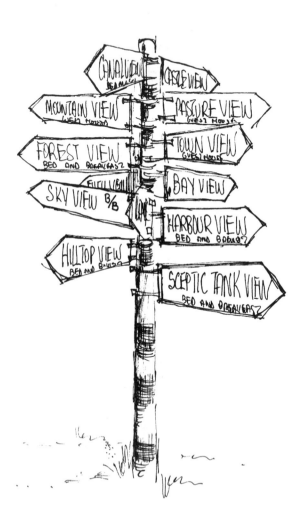

How To Use This Book

THIS BOOK IS arranged alphabetically, firstly by virtue of County names — County Cavan is followed by County Clare which is followed by County Cork, and so on — and then within the counties the individual entries are arranged alphabetically — so Longueville House, in north Cork, will follow after Lettercollum House, which is in south west Cork.

Entries in Northern Ireland are included in a separate section. The maps in the book are intended only as a general guide and we recommend that they be used in conjunction with an accurate Ordnance Survey map.

All visits to the Hotels, B&Bs and Country Houses included in this book were made anonymously. All accommodation was paid for and any offers of discounts or gifts were refused.

In cases where we felt the hospitality, comfort and service in a particular premises was of such a special, indeed unique, stature, we have marked the entry with a ★.

In cases where we felt the hospitality, comfort and service was especially enjoyable we have marked the entry with a ➡, meaning that it is worth making a detour in order to stay there.

Accommodation which we that we think offers outstanding value for money is marked with the symbol £.

Many of the Country Houses and B&Bs featured in this book are only open during the summer season, which means that they can be closed for any given length of time between October and March.

All prices and details apply to 1994 and are correct at the time of going to press. Should the circumstances of any of the entries change, however, we are unable to accept any responsibility .

Finally, we greatly appreciate receiving reports, suggestions and criticisms from readers.

The Bridgestone Awards

STARRED ACCOMMODATION ★

Ballymaloe House, Shanagarry, Co Cork
Hilton Park, Scotshouse, Co Monaghan
Norman Villa, Strandhill, Co Galway
The Old Presbytery, Kinsale, Co Cork
The Park Hotel, Kenmare, Co Kerry
Temple House, Ballymote, Co Sligo

ACCOMMODATION WORTH A DETOUR ➡

Assolas Country House, Kanturk, Co Cork
Chestnut Lodge, Monkstown, Co Dublin
Longueville House, Mallow, Co Cork
Mainistir House, Kilronan, Aran Island, Co Galway
Number Thirty-One, Dublin, Co Dublin
Saint Ciaran's, Kilronan, Aran Islands, Co Galway
Salville House, Enniscorthy, Co Wexford

ACCOMMODATION WHICH OFFERS
OUTSTANDING VALUE FOR MONEY £

Castle Murray House, Ballykineely, Co Donegal
Norman Villa, Strandhill, Co Galway
Number Thirty-One, Dublin, Co Dublin
The Old Presbytery, Kinsale, Co Cork
Bríd Poíl, Inis Oir, Aran Islands, Co Galway
Sea Court, Butlerstown, Co Cork
Seven North Mall, Cork, Co Cork
Temple House, Ballymote, Co Sligo

Introduction

IT MAY SEEM less than politic to mention the factor that unites the one hundred entries in this book. Indeed, for the people concerned, it may seem less than polite, and far from reassuring, and certainly not the kind of thing they want to hear. But, whenever one thinks about it, the conclusion is inescapable. The people in this book run establishments of every manner and style, in every category of comfort and cost, but they are all unified by one factor: hard work.

There is no alternative to this essential ingredient, if you wish to run an establishment which has character and charm, which gives value for money, which is one of the best places to stay in Ireland. Hard work, and nothing but hard work, will make a place to stay somewhere special. You need all the other factors, of course: a good aspect, a good eye for furnishings, the ability to cook intelligently and creatively. But, behind all this, there must be a personal animus which drives the person on.

This is the factor which modern hotels seem to have forgotten, or at least seem to believe is no longer necessary. They believe that large establishments can be run by rote, that if you have someone doing a job then that job will be done and, hopefully, will be done properly.

But the people in this book do not operate by this idea. Instead, their determination is not just that things should be done properly, but that they should be done in the very best way possible, the very best way imaginable. They contribute not just their efforts to the places they run, but also their character, their commitment. These one hundred places are characterised by hard work, and by personality.

There is also a rampant sense of intuition at play. The keeper of an hotel or a B&B or a country house needs to acquire what is, in effect, a seventh sense: the ability to predict the needs of a customer even before that customer can fully articulate just what it is they want. In this regard, modern, large hotels are much the same as modern, large supermarkets: they are expert at suggesting a wealth of choice, whilst actually selling you what it is they want you to buy. This may not be the same as what you actually want.

The places we choose to write about, on the other hand, are places which actually give you what you want. They can provide the comfort and the care, the hospitality and the assistance, because they do it on a personal level. And this is one of the happiest things to write about, and to discover, with places to stay in Ireland. The character of the people is paramount: they are the establishments. Not their specification — which will frequently be absurdly wide of the mark, or incapable of even suggesting the riches they can offer — or their price tag, or their position. The people are what count, and it is from their efforts that you get the things you actually want when you are on holiday, having a weekend break, touring with the family. They know what you want, because they know that you want the personal touch, the counsel of their experience, the calmness of their capability. The modern, bland hotel room is, in effect, the antithesis of the idea of hospitality. Uniform, regulated, cost-controlled, drained of all individuality, there is no room left in these places for a soul, for a human spark. What we try to find, in this one hundred places, are people who give of themselves, people who contribute the human touch, that lovely soft, gentle character which is so decisively Irish.

There is an enormous, added, bonus, when you find the sort of places which we seek out. They offer, no matter what price they may charge, exceptional value for money, for a simple reason. No one ever charges for being extra careful and thoughtful. No one ever charges for those little touches of generosity which make such a difference to staying in a place. You can charge for televisions and trouser presses; you can charge for direct-dial telephones and for king-size beds. But there will not be a supplement at the foot of the bill which says: 'Thoughtfulness and spontaneity carries a surcharge of 10%'. These things come free, and that is where you find value for money.

A correspondent wrote us a delightful letter during 1993, at the end of a cycling holiday around West Cork and Kerry in the course of which they sampled many different places to stay and to eat. Describing one of the places included in this book, he wrote 'Although the food was simple and the accommodation fairly plain, everything was done to a high standard and we thoroughly enjoyed ourselves. The hosts could not have been more welcoming. It goes to show that cost has little to do with true quality. It is that indefinable "something" that convinces you of true value for money'.

That indefinable 'something' is composed of hard work, personality and intuition. Despite their differences, this is what unites the people described in this book, that is what gives them their character, and what makes them such fine places in which to find yourself.

JOHN MCKENNA, SALLY MCKENNA
Durrus, Co Cork

B&B

LISNAMANDRA HOUSE
Crossdoney, Co Cavan Tel: (049) 37196
Bert & Iris Neill

The Neills' seventeenth century farmhouse is just south of the intricate complex of lakes of County Cavan's Erne System. Naturally enough, amongst others drawn by Lisnamandra's considerable reputation, the house attracts sodden fishermen who appreciate the early fortification of a Lisnamandra breakfast just as much as they welcome their return to comfortable rooms, an appropriate acreage of necessary towelling and tootsy-toasting electric blankets.

The list of options for breakfast in Bert and Iris's celebrated B&B seems to be as long as the 04 telephone directory, but a lot more interesting: porridge, black and white pudding, gammon, poached egg and waffles, scrambled eggs and mushrooms, pancakes and maple syrup; french toast and grilled tomato, grilled kippers on toast — on and on it goes, ending with the Falstaffian promise of: 'Any combination of the above'.

Open mid Apr-mid Oct
6 rooms, 4 en suite, 2 sharing 1 bathroom and 2 shower rooms
Average Price: £13 per person sharing, £14.50 en suite
No Extra Charges
No Credit Cards
Dinner for guests only, book by noon, £14
No Licence (bring your own)
No Wheelchair Access
Children — high chairs, cots
Varied Vegetarian options always available at breakfast
No pets
Enclosed Car Park
Lisnamandra House is clearly signposted on the Crossdoney Road leading from Cavan town.

Self-Catering Cottages
BALLYVAUGHAN RENTAL COMPANY
Ballyvaughan, Co Clare Tel: (065) 77029 Fax: 77181
Claire Walshe

Banish the dolorous, regretful nature of Frank Sinatra's 'A Cottage For Sale' from your consciousness and think, instead, of the promising charm of 'A Cottage For Rent'.

A cottage with an idyllic mien and location, near the sea, near to a bright little village with a good restaurant and with excellent pubs in which to while away the evenings, just right for romantic couples, even for friendly families. During the day you spend your time swimming or walking, or down by the harbour watching the boats.

You will find cottages like this, cottages for rent, on Claire Walshe's ever-expanding holiday rental list. Ms Walshe is as much of a landmark in the Ballyvaughan area of County Clare as Corkscrew Hill. A brilliant restaurateur and a whirlwind organiser and instigator, she runs a happy business whereby, if any local goes away for a while and wants to let their house, they tell Claire about it first. Beautiful, comfortable homes may only appear for a season on the list, but Claire will be the person to tell you about them. Availability varies from month to month, but you're likely to be offered a choice of thatched seaside cottages, perhaps grander country houses, or village centre apartments. One of the rental rooms is upstairs, over a post office.

So, if planning a romantic retreat for two, a billet for a family holiday, an autumn-break base or an Easter binge with all your sporty mates; if you want to hill walk in the Burren, study wild flowers, improve your Irish, or fish, or swim, then consult Claire and her Company, before you choose the roof you want over your own, and all those other, heads.

Open office hours all year round
Cottages rented Sat-Sat, priced per week (weekend deals in winter)
Credit Cards: Visa, Access
Wheelchair Access — in some houses
Pets only by special arrangement
In the tourist centre in Ballyvaughan (ask at Claire's restaurant if lost).

B&B with Restaurant
CAHERBOLANE FARMHOUSE
Corofin, Co Clare Tel: (065) 37638
Brid Cahill

The events of an extraordinary evening we spent in Caherbolane is
one of those stories on which we have dined out ever since, yet it
bears repetition, for it is so extraordinary as to almost beggar belief.
We arrived late at the house — little more than a standard, comfortable
but unremarkable big pile a few miles from the strangely weird village of
Corofin. We enjoyed a seriously divine dinner, cooked by Patricia Cahill
— spicy chicken wings with a just-right blue cheese dip, and some fried
potato skins to start. Then a pinky perfect slice of sirloin, and three
delicious lamb cutlets. Finally, a perfect chocolate and Grand Marnier
mousse, and sweet mince pies with a crème anglaise. A wonderful dinner.
The quality of the cooking was tremendous, but that is not the
extraordinary thing. The extraordinary thing was that after cooking
dinner, Patricia went home, then went into hospital and in the wee
small hours of the night she gave birth to a bouncing little boy.
It is this sort of sang froid, this effortless capacity to cope, which makes
Caherbolane work. By itself it is a very ordinary enough farmhouse,
just a quartet of unadorned rooms upstairs for guests and a dining
room below. But the energy and good cheer of the Cahills is addictive
and their calmness utterly remarkable. The fact that one can find such
sublime cooking in an area of Clare which is largely bereft of good
eating houses, makes it a perfect base from which to scoot around
the county, and somewhere to hurry home to for dinner.

Open all year
4 rooms sharing 2 shower rooms
Average Price: £13.50
No Service Charge
No Credit Cards
Dinner 7.30pm-9.30pm, £12 (also open to non-residents)
No Licence (bring your own wine)
No Wheelchair Access
Children — welcome
Always a Vegetariam dish of the day
No pets
Car park
Three miles outside Corofin on the road to Gort.

B&B
FERGUS VIEW
Kilnaboy, Corofin, Co Clare Tel: (065) 37606 Fax: (065) 37192
The Kelleher family

Mary Kelleher's house is a landmark for hospitality — that lovely, easy, capable, Clare hospitality which is so singular — and for fine, fine food. 'We're interested in food and cooking', says Mrs Kelleher, modestly, and her interest translates into attractive and wholesome food which it is famously easy to enjoy. The ravenous Burren walkers and lake fishermen, even idle car-bound travellers, who sit down for dinner at six thirty are in for a treat.

Mrs Kelleher's food is imbued with comforting grace notes, imbued with the desire to make a meal sustaining and enticing. Serene casserole of lamb with a honey and orange sauce, supported by simple, fresh celery and carrots. A steak of salmon cooked in parchment with Florence fennel. Vegetables and herbs have come from no further than the garden, so their vigour is bounteous.

Pavlova with fresh fruit and other fun, sticky desserts like lemon meringue pie are perfectly composed, leaving you the less-than-arduous task of muttering 'wonderful, wonderful' in response to the many enquiries as to whether everything is suitable and sufficient. Breakfast, meantime, offers another feast: crêpes with kiwi fruit and maple syrup; smoked kippers with tomato; a bumper breakfast of bacon with true free-range eggs.

The housekeeping in Fergus View is meticulous and the rooms extra comfortable: this is a homely house. From the moment of arrival, when you are served tea, and home-made jam with your scones, you will know that where you are is where you want to be.

Open Easter-1 Oct
6 rooms, 5 en suite
Prices: b&b £14 per person sharing, en suite £16, single supplement £5
No Extra Charges
No Credit Cards
Dinner for guests, book by noon
Wine Licence
No Wheelchair Access
Children — welcome
Vegetarian meals available (please give notice)
No pets
Enclosed car park
The house is on the right as you drive South to Kilnaboy.

B&B
ADÈLE'S BAKERY
Schull, Co Cork Tel: (028) 28459
Adèle Connor

The following story may sound apocryphal, may sound like a modern day rural myth, but it is true.

There was, once upon a time, a honeymooning couple. Still slightly tired from the exertions of the wedding, as all honeymooners are, they nevertheless had great plans for exploring the entire country — West Cork today, then off to Kerry, and then Galway!, and the Aran Islands and maybe Donegal if they had time, with a day or so in Dublin, right at the end.

They came to Schull in their little car, with their pair of bicycles fixed to the roof. They booked into Adèle's, a place best known as one of the best bakeries in the country, and now celebrated for the fine cooking which happens there in the evening. The building was, once upon a time, a bank. A simple quartet of rooms up the narrow stairs above the café, it's the kind of place that summons — somehow, someway — a youthful idea of freedom and lack of responsibility. Simple beds, simple boards on the floor, a shared bathroom, it fulfils the need for a functional, effective pensione, someplace from where you can stake out the pubs and eateries of Schull, a village of miniscule size and maximum fascination.

The honeymooners liked the look of it, liked the smell of baking, the scents of coffee, liked the prices. They booked for one night. Then, the next day, they decided to stay another night, maybe miss going to the Arans, maybe skip Dublin, at the end.

Two nights became three. Three became four.

They stayed, in all, for six nights. Bye-bye Kerry, and Galway, and everywhere else. They honeymooned, and ate and slept and had a whale of a time, in Schull, in Adèle's.

This story is true.

Open Apr-Nov, and three weeks at Xmas
4 rooms sharing shower and bathroom
Average Price: £12.50 per person, no single supplement
No Extra Charges
No Credit Cards
Restaurant open for dinner, £8-£15
Wine Licence
No Wheelchair Access
Children — high chair
Vegetarian meals available, and gluten free bread
No pets
Street Parking
On the main street in Schull, at the top of the hill.

Restaurant with Rooms
AHERNE'S
163 North Main Street, Youghal, Co Cork Tel: (024) 92424 Fax: (024) 93633
The Fitzgibbon family

There is a happy sense of timelessness about Aherne's. It may be
engendered by the fact that it is currently the third generation of
Fitzgibbons' who run this handsome place, but it may equally be the
true sense of professionalism and seriousness of purpose which the
family espouse and practice which makes the place ever-enduring.
Each and every year new followers are added to the fold of those for
whom the Fitzgibbon family's organisation spells bliss itself. Charmed
by the intimacy of the dining room, succoured by the comfort of the
food, lulled by the promise of the wine list and buffeted by the grand
charms of the bedrooms, they speak afterwards in enraptured tones,
these presidents, actresses, food journalists, visitors from abroad.
No-one, it seems, is immune to the charms of the pinky art-decked
dining room, or the cosy bar where you are left alone to drink in the
atmosphere, or the fine breakfasts in front of the fire on a brisk spring
morning, with fresh bread and good coffee and a fillet of fish which
you will find it difficult to forget for a long, long, time, such is its
succour and strength of flavour, its correctness. The comfort of the
rooms means that you scarcely notice the uninspiring views.

Open all year except Xmas week
10 rooms, all en suite
Average Price: £33.50 per person sharing, £44 single
No Extra Charges
Credit Cards: Visa, Access/Master
Restaurant (lunch £13.50, dinner £21), Bar and bar menus (from £5) available
Full Pub Licence
Wheelchair Access (incl disabled bathroom)
Children — cots, babysitting
Vegetarian meals with prior notice
No pets
Locked Car Park
On the main street in Youghal at the Waterford end of town.

Self-Catering Lodges

ARGIDEEN FISHING LODGES

Inchy Bridge, Timoleague, Co Cork Tel: (023) 46127 Fax: 46233
Tim Severin

Argideen means 'Little Silver Stream' and, at the stretch of the river which licks just past the fishing lodges, just up from Inchy Bridge, this quiet, secret water flows with quicksilver smartness, smoothly eliding the rocks and tree trunks which contain it. 'One guest, a photographer, actually saw a kingfisher one evening, and he was so delighted. Delighted just to see a kingfisher', says Tim Severin, who owns the four lodges.

The Argideen has been little-known, even amongst anglers, over the last decades. But, if you seek something with gills in place of wings, the river has been quietly providing locals from the fishery with sporting sea trout angling for years. One of the delights of staying here, aside from the proximity to one of the loveliest parts of Cork and the quirky, special restaurants which are local, is the fact that each lodge holds a Guest Rod, who is treated as a full member of the fishery during their stay. Time, then, to collect at dusk at Inchy Bridge with the few members of the fishery, and to parcel out the sea trout pools for the evening. Then, in appropriately silent communion, to take off to Wagners, or Bridge Pool, or Lorrigans, to wage wits and skill. During the day one can scour the Bandon, only 20 miles away, for salmon, or seek fish in both nearby lakes and at sea, for boats go out from Courtmacsherry in search of Blue Shark, Cod, Conger and Ling.

Meanwhile, back at the Lodge, there is easy comfort in the houses for kith and kin to enjoy, should they not be amongst the Brotherhood of the Barbour. The rooms are thoughtful, bright, carefully considered — you need only your own towels — and excellent value, especially in the low season.

Open Mar-Oct (Xmas by arrangement)
4 self-catering lodges, each sleeps 6 in 1 double bedroom plus 1 room with 4 full-size bunks
Average Price: £175-£375 per week
No fishing charges for guests
No Credit Cards
Fully fitted kitchen
Licence not applicable
No Wheelchair Access
Children — high seat, cot and babysitting service
Well-behaved pets accommodated
Car Park
Two miles outside Timoleague, signposted from the main road to Bandon.

Country House
ASSOLAS COUNTRY HOUSE ➥
Kanturk, Co Cork Tel: (029) 50015 Fax: (029) 50795
The Bourke Family

Assolas is dashingly romantic, at night when the house is dappled with
lights and you wander alongside the river and tiny bats career above,
splashing onto the surface of the water like bellyfloppers, or on a warm
morning, amidst the sprucely manicured hedges and shrubs, as you
maybe swing on the tree swing and think of your salad days. This is
one of those houses that fills you with pleasure at the very thought of
it, the very memory of a stay.

It is welcoming, thanks to Joe and Hazel Bourke and their assiduous and
assured youthful energy, their easy wit and style. Mrs Bourke cooks, and
she does so with a great feeling for both acuity of flavour and texture in a
dish, and adds an organic appreciation of how best to exploit the fresh
herbs, many of them grown out back in Assolas' vegetable garden and
plucked by Hazel herself. The torchy spice of rosemary will scent the jus
with a loin of lamb, garlic ramsons and the unfurled umbrella of a chive
flower will sit amidst a ring of salad leaves, elderflower will add a
muscatty bite to a soft gooseberry fool, a dish of batoned carrots will be
singing with the tastes of ginger and orange. In the mornings, Mr Bourke
turns his hand to breakfast, and Mr Bourke cooks a very fine breakfast.
Such wonderful food, enjoyed in the quiet comfort of the red-walled dining
room, makes you doubly glad to be at Assolas and, days after, images from
the visit come back into the mind: the whites-clad cook walking back
across the lawn after collecting herbs; the sea-green colour of a bowl of
asparagus soup; the bursting orange and red colours of a breakfast
compote; the lush comfort of the rooms. This country house makes sense,
enlivened as it is with the energy of young people giving something their
very best effort, and the clarion of comfort, relaxation and sophistication
one craves are found here. The rooms in the house are more expensive
than the rooms in the courtyard, and are worth the extra money.

Open 12 Mar-1 Nov
9 rooms, all en suite
Average Price: £40-£73 per person sharing, £50-£67 single
No Extra Charges
Credit Cards: Visa, Access/Master, Amex, Diners
Restaurant open for dinner, 7pm-8.30pm, £27, booking advisable
Full Licence
No Wheelchair Access
Children — welcome (early tea provided)
Vegetarian meals available on request
Facility for pets in the stables
Enclosed car park
Signposted from Kanturk.

Farmhouse

BALLYMAKEIGH HOUSE
Killeagh, Co Cork Tel: (024) 95184
Mrs Margaret Browne

'My girlfriend and I travelled to Ireland for Valentine's Weekend and we had a whopping great time at this gem of a place', writes a Mr McKenna from London — no relation, we hasten to add — before hitting overdrive in order to describe Margaret Browne's Ballymakeigh House. 'The house was so welcoming and warm with every comfort one would need, big fires, fresh flowers, crisp linen, rich and warm décor. The warm welcome even extended right through to the tea leaves'. All of this is completely true, utterly unarguable. But there is more. 'The food deserves a special mention. It all tasted so fresh, wonderful and light. I just happened to mention one morning that I love hot oysters and roast duck and that night that was exactly what Mrs Browne served to us for dinner — all at a very reasonable cost'. Unsurprisingly, Mr McKenna concludes: 'I shall definitely return there again'. Perhaps we should hold a convocation of McKennas at Ballymakeigh, Mr McKenna?

Open all year
5 rooms, all en suite
Average Price: £19 per person sharing, £24 single
No Extra Charges
No Credit Cards
Dinner, £17, book by 4.30pm
Wine Licence
No Wheelchair Access
Children — high seat, cot, babysitting service available
Vegetarian meals with notice only
No pets in bedrooms (except guide dogs)
Enclosed Car Park
Killeagh is between Midleton and Youghal on the N25: watch for the sign to the house on the road.

Country House
BALLYMALOE HOUSE ★
Shanagarry, Midleton, Co Cork Tel: (021) 652531 Fax: 652021
Myrtle & Ivan Allen

Approached on its own terms, Ballymaloe House will never fail
to please, to delight. If you let yourself fall captive to its quiet spell,
its peaceably instinctive way of functioning, then you will come to
understand how it has acquired its pre-eminent reputation in Ireland.
The rooms are designed, deliberately, to be simple, to reflect the fact
that you are in a country house and not an hotel. If the staff are young,
they are never less than charming, helpful. They, like everything else,
are an essential part of the Ballymaloe operation, and the key to this
house is the fact that they do things their own way. They do not ape
or imitate. These are the things which make Ballymaloe unique.
At breakfast the butter will be hand-churned, the porridge hand-roasted,
the eggs will come from the chickens who disport themselves with vigour
out back, and the bread — even the triangles of white toast — will have
been made that morning.
Dinner is a chapter in itself, even the less formal Sunday night buffet,
which amounts to little less than an homage to quality Irish ingredients
and an Irish way of cooking them. The wine list is good, surprisingly
inexpensive. The out-of-season weekend breaks are truly excellent value
Don't come to Ballymaloe expecting the accoutrements of the modern,
celebrated hotel — the rooms are not kitted out with every gadget and mod
con on the market, the staff do not fawn and flutter just because they are
dealing with people who may be wealthy or famous or whatever. Don't
expect the cooking to ape the creations of the culinary cutting edge — this
is farmhouse cooking. Enjoy it, instead, as a unique Irish establishment
that takes its place — on its own terms — amongst the finest places to eat
and stay anywhere in the world, and deserves to do so because it ploughs
such a dedicated, devoted and unique vision.

Open all year except 24-26 Dec
29 rooms, all en suite
Average Price: £55-£60 per person sharing, £75 single
No Extra Charges
Credit Cards: Visa, Access/Master, Amex, Diners
Restaurant open for lunch, £10, and dinner, £30
Full Licence
Wheelchair Access (downstairs rooms, but no disabled bathroom)
Children — welcome
Recommended for Vegetarians
No pets
Enclosed car park
Ballymaloe is signposted from the N25 Cork-Waterford road.

Country House
BALLYVOLANE HOUSE
Castlelyons, Fermoy, Co Cork Tel: (025) 36349 Fax: (025) 36781
Merrie and Jeremy Green

Ballyvolane sits comfortably and happily on the hillside at Castlelyons, quietly luxurious amongst quietly luxurious grounds, snuggled in amidst the infernally swollen charm of north east County Cork. This entire area is suffused with a meandering obliqueness, a relaxed and relaxing air of procrastination, nicely lazy sort of country.

Inside, the house is full of the right sort of burnished mahogany, and while portraits of long-gone ancestors glare down at you from the walls, anything ominous in their gaze is dissipated by the air of giddy, giggly fun which swaddles everyone staying here. The dinner party cooking, the bright fires, the gin and tonics: it's so appropriate it deserves to be satirised. Whilst there is much to admire everywhere throughout the house, the titanically deep baths in the front bedrooms are so gargantuan and epic they actually have to be stepped up to before you sink into. These are the rooms to go for: the others are excellent, but perhaps not so much fun, and being merry is the modus vivendi of Ballyvolane, a place where formality surrenders to warm feelings of comfort and humour.

Open all year except Xmas
6 rooms, 5 en suite, 1 with private bathroom
Average Price: £35-£44 per person sharing, £8 single supplement
No Extra Charges
Credit Cards: Visa, Access/Master, Amex
Dinner for guests, £20, book by noon
Wine Licence
Wheelchair Access
Children — high chairs, cots, babysitting
Vegetarian meals available
Pets welcome
Private Car Park
The house is very well signposted in the area and from the main road.

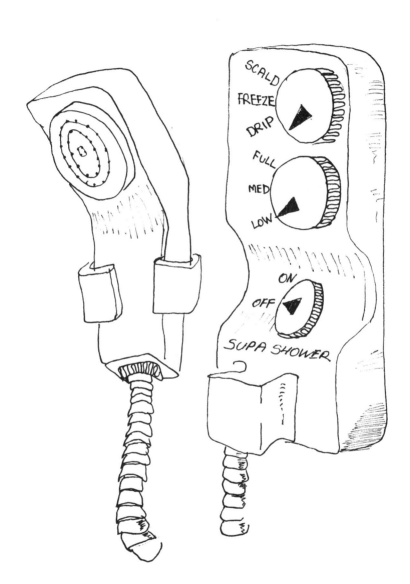

SCALD
FREEZE
DRIP
FULL
MED
LOW
ON
OFF
SUPA SHOWER

Country House
BANTRY HOUSE
Bantry, Co Cork Tel: (027) 50047 Fax c/o: 51417
Egerton Shelswell-White

Sitting high on the hill overlooking Bantry Bay and its littering of mussel bed bobbles, Bantry House is a serenely articulate architectural masterpiece. Right from the moment you arrive, it is a house which flatters your sense of well-being, flatters your sense of your own good taste. The wide-angle bedrooms suggest the space necessary for a Hollywood actress escaping paparazzi. The big broad beds suggest the necessity of congress, maybe even conception. And the confident aloneness, for this is the Marie Celeste of country houses, allows you to be your broody, self-obsessed best. Alone, perfectly alone.

There are, of course, people to meet and greet you at Bantry House. There is, in the morning, the elephantine roar of the trombone as Mr Shelswell-White struggles to coax a tune from his old dog'n'bone. There are likely to be droves and dozens of bus-borne tourists scouting around that part of the house which is nowadays a museum, and a perfectly droll museum at that. There may, if you are lucky, be a concert taking place in the library that very evening, some string quartet launching into Beethoven and Schubert with gusto, and a thronging audience sitting happily underneath a candlelit chandelier. But, if you wish to be alone and to evade string quartets and bus-borne travellers, you can hide away in the big rooms, maybe with a glass of grog you fixed yourself downstairs, and disappear into solipsism, into Garboesque grandness. All around the house things will be arranged, things will be operational, but they are done by unseen hands: the ship sails on, firmly commanded, but seemingly with no one at the helm.

Open all year, except Xmas period
6 double rooms, 1 suite, 2 adjoining family rooms sharing a bathroom
Average Price: Jan £40 per person, Mar-May & Oct-Dec £45 per person, Jun-Sept £50 per person, single supplement £10
No Extra Charges
Credit Cards: Visa, Access/Master, Amex
Dinner available to residents by special arrangement Mon-Fri, May-Oct (book by noon) £20
Wine Licence
No Wheelchair Access
Children — cots, family rooms
Vegetarian meals available (please give advance notice)
No pets
Enclosed car park
The gates of the house are clearly signposted just as you enter Bantry.

Self-Catering Accommodation
BLAIR'S COVE APARTMENTS
Durrus, Bantry, Co Cork Tel: (027) 61041
Renate Klotzer

In tandem with that treasure trove of good food which is the Blair's
Cove restaurant, the de Mey family also offer various sizes and shapes
of apartments around and about the group of Georgian stone houses
on this seaside estate just down the road from the quixotic little village
of Durrus, at the head of the Sheep's Head peninsula in West Cork.
Above the restaurant itself there is the Blair's Cove House Apartment.
Approached by an outside stone staircase, it consists of a double bedroom
with bathroom en suite and a studio room providing full kitchen and
dining space. There are comfortable chairs to settle into while overlooking
the glorious sunsets and dazzling daytime blues of Dunmanus Bay.
Blair's Cove House I and II are two apartments in the main house.
No I is a two storey apartment with two double bedrooms, plus shower
room upstairs, sitting room, dining room, kitchen downstairs. While
also on the first floor, No II is effectively a bed-sitting room with en
suite shower bathroom attached.
In the old smokery there is another two storey apartment, this time
with an en suite double, a twin and a bunk room and a separate shower
upstairs, and a sitting, cooking, dining area downstairs.
All the accommodation is kitted out to the same acute good taste as the
restaurant, and the location of the houses makes them perfect bases for
exploring not only central and west Cork with their plenitude of
culinary riches — this may be the best area of the entire country in
which to have a self-catering holiday — but also allow you to easily
scoot over the mountains into Kenmare and the charms of Kerry.

Open Mar-Oct
5 self-catering apartments sleeping 2-6
Average Price: from £130-£165 per week for apartments (sleeps 2), £235-£400 per
week for houses (sleep 4-6)
Extra Charges: electricity and final cleaning
No Credit Cards
Blair's Cove Restaurant open for dinner
No Wheelchair Access
Children — welcome (cots on prior notice)
No pets
Car park
1 mile from Durrus on the Durrus-Barleycove road.

Guesthouse
BOW HALL
Castletownshend, Co Cork Tel: (028) 36114
Dick and Barbara Vickery

Castletownshend has long been famous as the home of Edith
Somerville, of the ladylike scribbling duo Somerville and Ross, authors
of those winsome adventures of an Irish R.M. It is also the home of
what is perhaps the steepest main street in any village in Ireland.
Nothing too remarkable about a steep main street, perhaps, except
that this one has a fully grown tree sprouting out of the centre of the
road half way down the hill.

It is also home to Mary Ann's Bar, one of those cosy picturesque bars
so beloved of overseas guide books, where Patricia O'Mahony's food
has begun to establish a reputation for the upstairs restaurant.

But the coming star in Castletownshend is actually Barbara and Dick
Vickery's Bow Hall, a handsome late 17th century house on the right
hand side of the village near the top of that steep main street. There are
only three rooms, the style is a cosy country Americana, the greeting
and the food are fulsome and fine. Indeed, Mrs Vickery's muffins,
made maybe with blueberries, maybe with apple and bran, are fast
becoming Mrs Vickery's famous muffins. The sense of hide-away
comfort which the house wraps around the visitor suits this peaceful
little village to perfection.

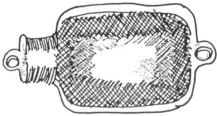

Open all year
3 double rooms
Average Price: £25-£28 per person
No Extra Charges
No Credit Cards
Dinner for guests, £18
No Wheelchair Access
Children — no facilities
Vegetarian meals on request
No Pets welcome
Private Car Park
In Castletownshend village centre.

B&B
CORTHNA LODGE
Schull, Co Cork Tel: (028) 28517
Loretta and Herbert Strickner

A mile or so outside the vivacious village of Schull, a place which has
a strong claim to be the food capital of Ireland such is the richness of
food on offer, Corthna Lodge exhibits all the grace notes of a house
where guests are destined to be thoroughly cared for.

The evident care in the design of the rooms in this modern house, with
their pastelly comfort and well-mannered charm, makes them cosy and
comfortable, especially so when the wind is whipping about outside, as
it is liable to do on this hill just south of Schull, as soon as summer
fades and autumn begins.

The gentleness and sweetness of Loretta and Herbert Strickner
themselves, and the attentive, tippy-toe air which they give to the house
compounds the pleasure of being here, as do the delicious breakfasts —
steaming coffee, fresh eggs and bread, handmade cheese from
Gubbeen farm just down the hill — setting up so well the ripe promise
of the day to come.

Corthna's skill is to combine the features of a special place — calm
comfort, warm welcome, careful cooking — and to bundle them into
a gift for the guest. 'When the bad weather hit Schull, Loretta gave us
electric underblankets, switched on her central heating and lighted
enormous fires in her sitting-room and brought us elevenses as we
waited for the weather to clear', wrote one correspondent, and you
think, yes, that's just what Loretta would do.

Open all year
6 rooms, all en suite
Average Price: per person sharing £20, single £25
No Extra Charges (laundry service £5)
No Credit Cards
No restaurant (but can book plenty in the locality)
No Licence
Wheelchair Access
Children — welcome
Vegetarian breakfast available
Pets accommodated
Enclosed car park
Corthna Lodge is signposted in Schull.

Cycling B&B

GABRIEL COTTAGE

Smorane, Skibbereen, West Cork Tel: (028) 22521
Suzanne Dark and Dominic Lee

Suzanne and Dominic's sweet little venture is better known as Irish
Peddlers, for they organise for their guests the dream and the gleam
of the open road, as seen from the saddle of a bike. You stay in either
the restored stone barn or in the house itself, set back from the loping
main road two miles or so before it arrives at the skittery town of
Skibbereen, in rooms that are sugar-sweet nice, kiddysome comfortable.
The rooms reflect 'our love of simple country style', they write, but this
undersings the dreamy nature of the barn rooms, and the dapper
perfection of the farmhouse.

You will get to know the house because super vegetarian meals —
aubergine parmigiana with pasta and seasonal salad; chick pea, garlic
and yogurt soup with brown bread; home made vanilla ice-cream with
blackberry coulis — are served around the big old table at the end of a
hard day hacking the roads of West Cork, and staunch breakfasts —
egg and mushroom scramble with fried soda bread; crêpes with fresh
fruit salad and fromage frais — will set you off at a fast pedal in the
morning. This deftly exotic area, of course, offers countless diversions
amidst its adorable little villages and its splendiferous pubs, should you
wish to eat out both at lunchtime and in the evening.

Suzanne and Dominic have a variety of cycle routes planned, bikes are
provided, waterproofs too, and there is a breakdown service should you
become stranded in some snug. For non-cyclists, rooms can often be
rented for shorter periods — you need to check in advance that this is
possible — and then Gabriel Cottage offers a superb, superb value base
for touring lovely West Cork. By car.

Open 30 Apr-30 Sept (B&B off season by prior arrangement)
2 double rooms, 1 twin, all en suite
Average Price: Cycling from £220 per person sharing, per week, B&B £16-£18 per
person sharing, single supplement for cycling £50
No Extra Charges
Credit Cards: Visa, Access/Master, Amex
Vegetarian dinner, £15, book by 10am
No Licence   No Wheelchair Access
Children — high chairs, cots (cycling for over 16s only)
Recommended for Vegetarians
Pets welcome, but not in rooms
Private Car Park
Gabriel Cottage is 2 miles east of Skibbereen, set back from the N71. (Coach service
from Cork will stop outside if requested)

B&B

GARNISH HOUSE

Western Road, Cork City, Co Cork Tel: (021) 275111 Fax: 273872
Hansi Lucey

The abbreviated Esperanto of the B&B business catapults into orbit on the Western Road, a busy slew of houses on the road from the southern capital out to Killarney and points West.

There is the promise, on a bright neon sign, of 'H & C, C.H., All Rooms', to tempt you, or 'B&B, Hot & Cold, Central Heating & Tea Making Facilities'. Which bit, you might ask, is it that runs hot and cold?

'En Suite Optional, Colour TV in all rooms' signally spells out a late-century sense of priority, while 'Hot & Cold, T.V.' rather makes the eyes water.

If all this shorthand sounds like so much Greek, then an evening in Hansi Lucey's Garnish House will have you composing your own Esperanto to Mrs Lucey's accomplishment of skills. 'Hospitality not Optional. Hot Never Cold. Charm Permanently on Tap. Endless Solicitude'. Okay, it may not fit onto a bug-eyed yellow sign, but it will be written on your heart.

Mrs Lucey was a nursing sister, and it is this she associates as her gift in the people business, though such decent friendliness is something instinctive, not something that can be learned. 'How are you? Did you sleep well? Were you comfortable? Would you like some more hot toast — it's on its way'. On and on it goes, this wonderful litany of welcomes and solicitations, more important than any volume of promised, abbreviated, services. The rooms in Garnish House are naturally cosy and contain all you might want, but it is the spontaneity, the lovely windy climb of those Cork accents — 'You' softened and abbreviated to the cushy 'Ye', which makes you right at home immediately — that makes Garnish such a fun place to be.

No Restaurant facilities (light snacks if required)
No Licence
No Wheelchair Access
Children — high seats, cots, babysitting service
Vegetarian breakfast always available (health food a speciality)
Pets accommodated
Locked Car park
The Western Road is the beginning of the road to Killarney.

Hostel
ISAAC'S HOSTEL
48 MacCurtain Street, Cork City Tel: (021) 500011 Fax: 506355

Isaac's is the kind of place where, as you lie on your bed on a warm
afternoon, the sound of some trumpeter playing some cool jazz may
come quietly drifting across the quad and you will ask yourself: just
who was he, that young man that you once were? Of those things
which should be compulsory in life — good white Burgundy at
affordable prices, the works of M.F.K. Fisher and Elizabeth David,
annual visits to Paris and, if we are talking about trumpeters, a set of
all Miles Davis' recordings — every city and town should also boast a
hostel which is as sassy, as smart and as essential as Isaac's Hostel in
MacCurtain Street.

Housed in a beautiful old mill building which has been refurbished
with imagination and good taste, it is comfortable, clean, cheap and
has an air of vitality and sang froid which makes it a vital, groovy place
to spend the night. The rooms, from basic dormitories to the smaller
4/6 bed dorms, to the twin and double rooms and the family rooms, are
clean and simple, their narrowness offset by generous height, and are
altogether closer in style to a European pensione than the standard,
dreaded Irish hostel.

The stairs and corridors are bright and imaginative, there are art
posters on the walls (though the bedrooms could do with some), doors
feel solid and close reassuringly, the bathrooms are that super-smart
set-up where the room becomes a shower room when necessary.
Towels and linen are clean and good-quality.

Breakfast enjoys the miracle of good coffee and decent bread
downstairs in the Studio, where you can eat the simple food sold here
or cater for yourself in the kitchen. You can, of course, opt for the
snazzier event which is a meal in the Brasserie at the front of Isaac's,
and let the animation and ambition which fuels this entire organisation
make you feel young once again.

Open all year round
The hostel sleeps 220 in total, divided up into 10/16 bed dorms, 4/6 bed dorms,
family rooms (5 bed), double, twin and single.
Prices per person: dorms £5.50-£7.50, twin £13.50, single £18.50. Family room
(sleeps 5) £44
No Extra Charges
Credit Cards: Access/Master, Visa
Hostel kitchen for residents plus Brasserie
Wine Licence
Wheelchair access — disabled bathroom, lift
Children welcome   Vegetarian food available
No pets
Car park arrangements made with nearby car park
Cork city centre, just north of the river.

Restaurant with Rooms

LARCHWOOD HOUSE

Pearson's Bridge, nr Ballylickey, Co Cork Tel: (027) 66181
Mr & Mrs Vaughan

Larchwood is, first and foremost, a family home. Unusually for a family home, however, it just happens to have a restaurant, and happens to have four rooms upstairs for guests. The lounge, then, is also the sitting room, whilst the dining room is simply a larger than usual family dining room, with various tables arrayed around the walls, some with a splendid view of the splendid garden.

Sheila Vaughan is an expert cook and a well-crafted skill runs right through her kitchen work, producing elegant terrines, baked avocado, lamb's liver with orange and Dubonnet as starters, soups which are fresh and flavoursome, then crisp sorbets. The principal distinction of main courses, whether one chooses fish or meat, is not only their persuasive fulsomeness, but the fulsomely enormous portions: dinner at Larchwood amounts to a feast, a feast which the richly sinful desserts bring to a rousing climax.

If you object to any manner of a domestic atmosphere when dining out, then Larchwood is unlikely to appeal. But, if the thought of only having to climb upstairs to bed after a boozy dinner sounds like just the sort of intensive relaxation you feel you need, then Larchwood, in its unlikely way, may furnish what you crave.

Open all year, except Xmas
4 rooms, all en suite
Average Price: £20 per person
No Extra Charges
Credit Cards: Visa, Access/Master, Diners
Restaurant open from 6.30pm, £22
Wine Licence
No Wheelchair access
Children — over 12 years welcome
Vegetarian meals provided with advance notice
No pets
Enclosed car park
Signposted from the Ballylickey/Glengarriff road.

Hostel
LETTERCOLLUM HOUSE
Timoleague, Co Cork Tel: (023) 46251
Con McLoughlin & Karin Austin

Strategies for happiness when at Lettercollum House.
Firstly, infants, toddlers and others who may be still at the food-flinging rather then food-swallowing stage, can be fed and watered in the hostel kitchen of the house, before being quartered upstairs in your family room. You then peel off your goo-encrusted T-shirt, pump up your hair, and head downstairs. No need for a babysitter, no need to worry, no need to drive anywhere. You are looking for wonderful food? So walk downstairs.

Unfortunately, the agonising part of the evening is just about to begin. Tonight, will it be free range chicken braised with onion marmalade? Breast of duck with plum and cardamom sauce? A salad of smoked chicken and sun-dried tomatoes? With all this agonising, it sure is a good thing you don't have to worry about those sprogs of yours, dreamily snoozing away upstairs.

If the kids are past the food-flinging stage, then there is no better place to introduce them to the disciplines of the table than Lettercollum. Fortysomethings with adolescents in tow and a Haight Ashbury echo in their memories will enjoy the vaguely hippyish style and informal, relaxed vibe of the house. For Sunday lunches, with grannies and grandkids and anyone else in between, this is one of the nicest spaces in which to enjoy lunch, and glorious food such as squid cooked in red wine with tagliatelle, crab quiche with yogurt and fennel sauce or those great staples like leg of lamb with garlic and a tarragon cream sauce or pot roasted loin of pork, is absurdly inexpensive.

Prices for accommodation are extremely low, rooms are no more than functional, but this, of course, allows for more spending on the superb food, and more inquiry in the direction of a short but interesting wine list.

Open Mar-Nov
Average Price: dorms from £5.50, other accommodation £8-£12
Extra Charges: £1 laundry charge if using house laundry in dorms. (Free for private rooms)
Credit Cards: Visa, Access/Master
Restaurant open from 7.30pm, from £17.50 (£7.50 vegetarian hostel menu available) Breakfast £2-£3. Self-catering kitchen
Wine Licence
No Wheelchair Access
Children — cots, tree house
Recommended for Vegetarians
No pets
Enclosed car park
Lettercollum House is just outside Timoleague and clearly signposted.

Country House
LONGUEVILLE HOUSE ➡
Mallow, Co Cork Tel: (022) 47156 Fax: (022) 47459
The O'Callaghan family

In Longueville, the O'Callaghan family strive to achieve a degree of
self-sufficiency which is dauntingly impressive. Their own lamb, most
of their own vegetables from their own gardens. Salmon from the
Blackwater river. A small collation of wine made every year from the
Muller-Thurgau grape. Why, William O'Callaghan has even begun to
hunt for truffles around and about the trees of the estate.
This is a fine and important thing, for Mr O'Callaghan is one of the
finest cooks in the country, a man able to extract and conjure the most
exquisite tastes from the ingredients at his disposal. His prowess,
indeed, has meant that Longueville is now famed more as a
gastronomic temple than a straightforward country house. Like nearby
Assolas, this is a vision of the country house which fuses the efficiency
and assurance of an hotel with the family personality of a country
house. Others try to glide by on charm and simple offerings of food:
Longueville has the charm, and food of exquisite complexity.
Jane O'Callaghan — William's mother, and Aisling — William's wife,
form a wonderful double team, the former inexhaustibly loquacious,
the latter reserved and helpful. There is nothing about County Cork as
to which they cannot advise you in order to get the very best from the
place, and when you return to Longueville they set a tone of
competence and comfort which is immediately disarming. Breakfasts
are amongst the best in the country, with homemade blood puddings,
sprightly eggs, sweet bacon.

Open mid Mar-late Dec
16 rooms, all en suite
Average Price: from £51 per person
No Extra Charges — special 2 and 3 day rates available
Credit Cards: Visa, Access/Master, Amex, Diners
Restaurant open for lunch £15, dinner £26
Full Pub Licence
No Wheelchair Access
Children — high chairs, cots
Recommended for Vegetarians
No pets
Private Car Park
Longueville House is about 3 miles out of Mallow on the N22 Killarney Road.

B&B

LYNWOOD

Schull Road, Ballydehob, Co Cork Tel: (028) 37124
Mrs Ann Vaughan

Lynwood is very much a house in the Irish suburban style, a place
where no surface is left untouched, unstyled, unelaborated, unadorned,
a place where a generous excess dominates. Everything beams bright
as a button, and the buttons in this comfortable house are ornate and
brassy, polished, buffed, spit-and-shined. Every surface area is busy
with colours and elaborations, a kaleidoscope of designs, a wealth of
detail almost to the point of delirium. The housekeeping is as
meticulous as the elaboration, the welcome is friendly and the location
ideal for overnighting when scooting around this darling village in this
loveliest part of West Cork.

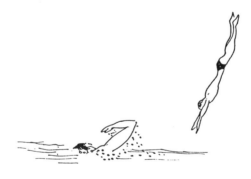

Open Apr-Oct
3 bedrooms all en suite
Average Price: £14-£15 per person (£18 single)
No Extra Charges
No Credit Cards
No Dinner
No Licence
No Wheelchair Access
Children — welcome
Vegetarian breakfast always available
Pets accommodated
Car park
No function rooms
Just up the hill in Ballydehob, driving towards Schull you will see the sign on your right.

B&B
THE OLD BANK HOUSE
Kinsale, Co Cork Tel: (021) 772968/774075
Marie Reise

A handsome, town-centre B&B in a building that was, once, the Munster and Leinster Bank, The Old Bank House is an oasis of cool sanity, somewhere that seems especially valuable during holiday times when Kinsale can appear to be on the brink of overheating on an hourly basis.

The trappings of the modern age are all here: direct dial telephones, multi-channel TV, big, elegant bathrooms, but Michael and Marie Reise never allow the house to sink into formulaic blandness, and they strive annually for changes and for improvements, features which will make the house more complete, more composed.

Open all year except Xmas
9 rooms, all en suite
Average Price: £26-£50 per person sharing, £35-£45 single
No Extra Charges
Credit Cards: Visa, Access/Master, Amex
Dinner available at the Reises' restaurant
Wine Licence
No Wheelchair Access
Children — no facilities
Vegetarian meals with 24 hours notice
No pets
Street Parking
Kinsale town centre.

B&B

THE OLD PRESBYTERY ★ £

Cork Street, Kinsale, Co Cork Tel: (021) 772027
Ken & Cathleen Buggy

Everything you encounter in Ken and Cathleen Buggy's Old Presbytery
has a purpose. Everything works to add meaning and character to the
house, everything conspires to build an aesthetic, to add an extra patina
of personality, to contribute something witty, something humorous.
The beautiful hand operated printing press which cradles a selection
of books. That great big wicker linen basket. The smooth round of the
butter churn. Mr Buggy's paintings and streetscapes which decorate
the walls, the clever cartoons he has drawn that have you chuckling
away to yourself with mirth, years after you first saw them, when the
memory of one of them rushes back into the mind. The fascinatingly
useless pulp novels. The fabulously baleful big brass beds with their
come-hither softness and crisp sheets of snowy-white.
It may sound eclectic and uncritical but, assembled all in one place,
these artefacts construct a house which is marvellously articulate,
which reveals an eye devoted to correctness, to putting the right thing
in the right place, to finding the right thing for the right place. The
Chinese have an expression for this consideration as to the layout
and physical well-being of a room — Feng Shui — a concept which
expresses the belief that the organisation of a room greatly affects
personality and good fortune. The Old Presbytery will greatly influence
your character and good fortune: you will be over the moon to find
yourself here, and hardly able to believe your luck.
Ken and Cathleen complete this spatial paragon, with Mr Buggy's
breakfasts never anything less than perfect — the soda bread crumbly,
the porridge a smooth fougasse of oats and cream, the eggs fresh, the
bacon smoky — and Mrs Buggy as calm, collected and charming as
you wish you were yourself.

Open all year except Xmas period (open New Year)
6 rooms, 4 en suite
Average Price: £20 per person sharing, £30 single
No Extra Charges
No Credit Cards
Dinner by arrangement only
Wine Licence
No Wheelchair Access
Children — no facilities
Vegetarian breakfast always available
No Pets
Enclosed car park
Just at the corner of Cork Street, opposite the church.

B&B
RODEEN
Castletownbere, Co Cork Tel: (027) 70158
Ellen Gowan

Ellen Gowan's bright, light and airy bungalow overlooks Bere Island,
but before you stretch your gaze to the horizon, there is first the
pleasure of inspecting the beautifully maintained and cared-for shrubs
and plants in the almost sub-tropical garden. Mrs Gowan, one of those
inexhaustible women who manages to do two jobs better than you can
do one, also runs a garden centre as well as this most well-regarded
B&B, so her home is home to a splendiferous array of plant life.
She also cooks with fine discrimination, cleverly using the flowers from
the garden to garnish her work, and conjuring a splendid selection of
fresh fruit and fresh scones, porridge and local cheeses, traditional
breakfasts and well-judged surprises. Eaten in the conservatory, with
the balm of Mrs Gowan's attentiveness on hand to spoil you, it is a fine
thing indeed.

Open all year except Xmas
5 double rooms, en suite
Average Price: £15 per person
No Extra Charges
No Credit Cards
Dinner by arrangement (book by noon)
No Licence
No Wheelchair Access
Children welcome
Vegetarian meals available on request
No Pets
Private Car park
Signposted from the Glengarriff road.

Country House
SEA COURT £
Butlerstown, Bandon, Co Cork Tel: (023) 40151 (Caretaker Tel: 023 40218)
David Elder

The light around this area of Cork shades everything it touches in pastel colours, graces the day with a marshmallowy gentleness, an intricate impressionism which, on warm summer days as you wend and wind around the softly inclined roads, lends a certain light headedness to how one sees this quiet, often overlooked part of County Cork. Only the sea itself can break the peace that it generates. And in this environment the fine house that is Sea Court sits colourfully oblique, a place which has the mute confidence of a long history. David Elder himself seems to fit perfectly in these surroundings. A quiet-spoken, cultured American, he oversees all aspects of the house from the careful cooking to the authoritative renovation of its five colourful bedrooms, painted in Wedgewood blues, fudgey terracotta, a cheeky Papal purple, colours which soak up the light and, in the big, breezy bedrooms, create the impression of hugely generous space. Furnishings in all the rooms are happily sparse — no nonsensical clutter — and the total effect is nothing less than uplifting. Absorb deep lungfuls of the clean, clean air and you are unlikely to need any other sort of nightcap.

Breakfasts and dinners are simple and correct, fine value, completing the profile of articulate restraint which drives you back to the soft sensibility of Sea Court.

Open mid Jun-mid Aug (available for self catering the remainder of the year. Enquire with the caretaker)
5 double rooms, 4 en suite
Average Price: £18.50 per person sharing, £21.50 single.
No Extra Charges
No Credit Cards
Dinner by arrangement (book by noon)
No Licence
No Wheelchair Access
Children — welcome
Vegetarian meals available on special request
Pets accommodated in out buildings
Car park
Signposted from Butlerstown.

Hotel
SEA VIEW HOUSE HOTEL
Ballylickey, Co Cork Tel: (027) 50073 Fax: 51555
Kathleen O'Sullivan

'I thought they were going to give me a big hug when I walked in', a friend said of Sea View, and if you did indeed get a big hug it wouldn't seem so unusual, it might just seem right, rather nice, actually, for sweet embraceable you.

The effortless attention and inherent kindness of the staff is the secret that makes Sea View so charming. They do things right, not as the result of rigid training or autocratic management, but simply from an instinct for good manners and care. That sentiment, that instinct, underlies everything that happens in Sea View, making it a special hotel.

People come to Kathleen O'Sullivan's innocent and mildly old-fashioned hotel, a couple of miles outside of Bantry on the road to Glengarriff, to have a good time, to celebrate the special events and days of their lives, and they celebrate them with gusto, with determination to wring the best possible memories from the day that is in it. The staff, those huggable folk, are as determined as you that you should have the best possible time.

The food these huggable youngsters bring to the table, both at breakfast and, especially, at dinner, is so delicious, so buttery and creamy, that you forget your concern for artery and waistline: never mind comfort food, these dishes transport you all the way back to the womb, caress you tenderly, you sweet embraceable you.

Open mid Mar-mid Nov
18 rooms, all en suite
Average Price: £30-£40 per person sharing low season, £32-£50 high season
No Extra Charges
Credit Cards: Visa, Access, Amex
Restaurant open for dinner, £21 + 10%
Full Licence
Wheelchair Access
Children — welcome
Vegetarian meals always available
Pets accommodated (not in public rooms)
Enclosed car park
Signposted on the N71 as you drive into Ballylickey.

Guesthouse
SEVEN NORTH MALL £
7 North Mall, Cork Tel: (021) 397191
Angela Hegarty

Whilst this handsome town house, down towards the end of the river malls in Cork city, has the standard requisites for the business traveller — the 'phone, the TV, the trouser press, the hairdrier, the luggage horse — it is no bland, anodyne shack-up for suits. 7 North Mall is valuable because of the cool, understated air it possesses, something which makes it operate — almost — as a retreat in the bubbling, busy city of Cork.
The air of understatement is seen in the appreciation of the importance of carefully chosen furnishings, carefully chosen utensils, carefully chosen addendums. Breakfast, thus, is a chance to peruse the papers which are left out, though the expertise of properly scrambled eggs is likely to demand your attention more stringently than any amount of news or gossip. Good coffee from a cafetiére, real orange juice and the gritty, warming tactility of Stephen Pearce crockery makes the meal truer, deeper.
There are chairs to lounge in, baths to submerge in and an evident attention in the housekeeping. The blankness and dull functionalism which annihilates any sense of comfort in the modern hotel where business folk might normally stay is absent here, and the tired worker can relax in a genuine, real environment, whilst the traveller is likely to revel in it.
The location of the house means that everywhere in the city is proximate, and walkable, especially some of Cork's best restaurants. For anyone arriving on the ferry at Cork it offers secure parking and an excellent first-night, last-night location.

Open all year except Xmas
5 rooms, all en suite
Average Price: £25 per person sharing, £35 single (£180 per week)
No Extra Charges
Credit Cards: Visa, Access
No evening meal provided (plenty of excellent restaurants nearby)
No Licence
Wheelchair Access
Children — no facilities
Vegetarian breakfast available
Pets (by arrangement)
Locked Car Park
On the riverfront in Cork city.

Guesthouse
SCILLY HOUSE INN
Scilly, Kinsale, Co Cork Tel & Fax: (021) 772413
Karin Young & Bill Skelly

It is easy , if one has a mind to build a luxury B&B, to simply throw money in the direction of your idea and to hope that a shower of cash will buy you the sort of good taste which discriminating guests will seek out.

Easy, but almost certainly doomed to failure, as certain large houses which have been built as B&Bs in Kinsale attest to. To create a luxury B&B needs, firstly, a sense of the place and importance of beauty, and the ability to make this beauty both tactile and, vitally, accessible. Karin Young's Scilly House, just out of Kinsale on the Scilly side and perched on the hill peering across the harbour, is a place that solves the problem of accessible good taste and an envelopment of beauty, seemingly effortlessly.

The rooms are vast, and vastly comfortable but never overstated: the colours in the traditional quilts and the furnishings play with light and space and easily accommodate the rafts of bright light which come hurling through the windows, bouncing back from the sea. One room is actually in a cottage set fast by the house. Downstairs there is, again, subtlety and understatement, things left to speak for themselves. The understatement, it must be said, meets its Waterloo when it comes to the baths, which are gargantuan and, it appears from even the briefest skiffle through the rather fruity visitors' book, irresistible to one and all, all together. Whether you arrive with wishes of water-borne romance, on the sea or in a tub, or prefer to keep your feet firmly on the ground, this is a romantic house, its attractions always evident, but ready to dissolve in a gaze. Breakfasts are excellent.

Open mid Apr-Oct
6 rooms and 1 cottage, all en suite
Average Price: from £40 per person sharing, £65 single
No Extra Charges
Credit Cards: Visa, Access/Master, Amex
Evening meals for pre-booked groups only
Wine Licence (wine bar downstairs)
No Wheelchair Access
Children — over 8 yrs only (£15 sharing suite rooms)
Vegetarian breakfast always available (fresh fruit, omelettes etc)
No pets
Enclosed car park
Scilly House is just around the corner from Man Friday Restaurant.

B&B with Restaurant

TRAVARA LODGE

Courtmacsherry, Co Cork Tel: (023) 46493
Mandy Guy

Travara Lodge sits looking out on the sea in the beautiful, pastel-painted village of Courtmacsherry, and Mandy Guy works hard to make a success of both the little restaurant downstairs and the rooms upstairs. The food she prepares in the evenings is simple and inviting — warm smoked salmon with cucumber and dill; sole layered with prawns and baked; meringues with fresh fruit— and it's always fine value, as is the short but quaffable selection of wines she culls from Galvin's in Cork. The rooms have pummeling showers and comfortable beds and those at the front of the house have super views across the calm inlet with its baby-blue water and baby-blue sky. These are the rooms to chase after.

'With advance notice we do our best to accommodate any requests, i.e. ground floor room, cots, baby sitters, sea view, dogs, vegetarian meals, packed lunch, early breakfast etc', they say, and they do mean it. The simple, but valuable, desire to please, and the desire to help one to make a good time even better, is what motivates Ms Guy and powers the hospitality of Travara Lodge.

Don't worry, by the way, should you fear that Courtmacsherry might prove to be as twee in spirit as one might imagine from its slightly kiddy-book appearance. The loveliness of the village conceals a more-than-slightly-wild streak amidst the locals: weigh in for the Courtmacsherry Shrimp Festival in September, when the Hilarious Shrimp Cookery Competition slugs it out with a Shrimp Spitting Competition (how do you teach a shrimp to spit?) and when local cooks and producers combine to present their wares, and you will see the place at its best.

Open Mar-Oct
7 rooms, all en suite
Average Price: £17.50 per person sharing, £15 single
No Extra Charges — 10% discount for 1 week's booking
Credit Cards: Visa, Access/Master
Restaurant open for dinner, £15-£18
Wine Licence
Wheelchair Access — one en suite ground floor room
Children — high chairs, cots, babysitting
Vegetarian meals available (a speciality of Mondays)
Pets accommodated on special request
Private Car Park
Just on the waterfront in Courtmacsherry.

Country House

ARDNAMONA HOUSE & GARDENS

Lough Eske, Donegal, Co Donegal Tel: (073) 22650
Amabel & Kieran Clarke

This is an impossibly beautiful place, with the Blue Stack mountains cradling the eager waters of Lough Eske. Amabel and Kieran Clarke's house sits fast in the wrap of lough and forest, and the bloom of rich summer greens and blues is matched by the shocking russet vividness of the ferns in the winter. You can walk and drive around and about the lake and feel you are miles from anywhere remotely civilised: in fact, Donegal town, with its somewhat less serene charms, is about ten minutes away.

Ardnamona has one of the oldest collections of tree rhododendrons in Ireland and, whilst their multifarious multiplicity may be of absorbing interest to botanists, for the non-specialist it is their atmospheric effect, swooping and drooping all around the gardens of Ardnamona, which creates an atmosphere somewhere between the petrified forest and the enchanted forest.

There are five rooms in the house, south facing and brightly pastelly, and a self-catering cottage in the rear yard which can sleep four. Mrs Clarke used to cook professionally, and the assurance of professional skills means that one looks forward, with relish, to dinner, a blessing for the traveller in County Donegal, which remains a county largely denuded of good food. You may find, however, that the 100 acres of Ardnamona and its frontage onto the lough is as much of the county as you will want to explore.

Open all year except Xmas and New Year
5 rooms, 2 en suite, 3 with private bathrooms
Average Price: £25-£30 per person
No Extra Charges
Credit Cards: Visa, Access/Master
Dinner for guests £15, book by noon
Wine Licence
No Wheelchair Access
Children — high chairs, cots, babysitting
Vegetarian meals with prior notice
Dogs allowed, but not in bedrooms
Private Car Park
Follow the signs to Harvey's Point, the house is two miles further down that road.

Country House
CASTLEGROVE HOUSE
Letterkenny, Co Donegal Tel: (074) 51118

Sitting hard on the shores of splendid Lough Swilly, a few miles outside the doleful, severe town of Letterkenny, Castlegrove operates principally as a guest house, with big, comfortable bedrooms painted in relaxed dark hues. In the evenings, however, Castlegrove also operates as a restaurant, with both ravenous residents and hungry locals making their way here in search of huge helpings of food. The menu is expansive and maybe a little too much so: it is perhaps wisest to stick with some grilled meat to accompany a good baked potato and a decent bottle of red wine to make up a good dinner, though desserts are well realised.

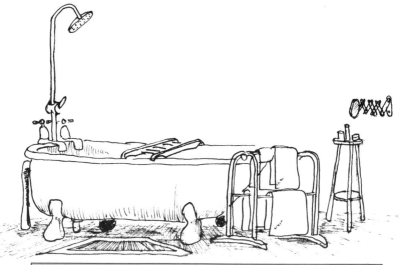

Open all year except Xmas period and mid Jan
7 rooms, 6 en suite
Average Price: per person sharing, low season £25 high season £35
No Extra Charges
Credit Cards: Visa, Access, Amex
Dinner for guests £17, book by noon
Full Licence
No Wheelchair Access
Children — cots and babysitting
Vegetarian meals available (please give notice)
Pets welcome
Enclosed car park
Between the two roundabouts in Letterkenny, you will see the sign for the house.

Restaurant With Rooms
CASTLE MURRAY HOUSE £
St John's Point, Dunkineely, Co Donegal Tel: (073) 37022
Thierry and Clare Delcros

You could come to Castlemurray with nothing more in mind than to
feast on Thierry Delcros' superb food, but before you can pay attention
to M. Delcros' cooking you will first have to drag your raptured gaze
away from some of the most astonishingly gorgeous views you will find
anywhere in Ireland. In wintertime the light moving across the bay dies
slowly, leaving a smudge of spectral light on top of the hills which is
echoed by the lapping fringe of the waves. In summer the golds and
blues are mesmerising, always changing. The gentleness of the house,
the element of softness about its character, is doubly comfortable in
the midst of the hard relentlessness of Donegal.
Castlemurray has become a very cultish place in the last couple of years,
particularly amongst Northerners who can scoot across to this spot just
a few miles west of Donegal town here in no time whatsoever. The cooking
is a virtuoso demonstration of how Irish foods — a local bio-dynamic
farmer, Thomas Becht, produces many of the ingredients used here — and
French skills are perfect platefellows. The duck pâté salad; profiteroles
stuffed with crab meat, served with a soupçon of spicy tomato confit;
crispy lobster portioned and served in a pillow of filo pastry; stuffed chicks
with pommes boulangere and crisp red cabbage. Desserts are as heavenly
with flavour as everything else: the crisp bite of cassis in an ice, the
yielding milkiness of a brûlée or a caramel. In the morning, breakfast is
especially fine, for M. Delcros has fully got to grips with the Irish breakfast
of bacon and eggs and gives it a sharply realised European tweaking.
The rooms in Castle Murray are comfortable, suitable: perfect for
overnighting, but also suitable for a longer stay, though the house gets
very quiet during the day. Do not expect an effusive Irish welcome,
however: this is a restaurant with rooms and the focus is on the
restaurant, so guests effectively look after themselves.

Open all year (except 24-26 Dec)
10 rooms, all en suite
Average Price: £22 Jun-Sep, £18 low season per person sharing, £26 single
No Extra Charges
Credit Cards: Visa, Access
Restaurant open dinner £16-£20
Full Licence
No Wheelchair Access
Children — welcome
Vegetarian meals available (please give notice)
Small Pets by arrangement (not in bedrooms)
Enclosed car park
Castle Murray is signposted just after the village of Dunkineely,
on the road to Bruckless.

B&B
KNOCKALLA FARM
Ballynashannagh Tel: (074) 59105
Tim Spalding & Norah Newell

Way, way up the gorgeous Fanad peninsula, but adroitly adjacent
to the road as it courses through this chauvinistically beautiful
countryside, is Knockalla, a handsome farmhouse announced by
the happy field of organically grown vegetables which stretches
enticingly out in front of it.

Tim and Norah offer Bed and Breakfast — there are four rooms in the
main house and a further three in a converted wing — and also evening
meals, specialising in wholefoods and using their own organic produce
— the owners themselves are vegetarian, but are happy to cater for
non-vegetarians on request. So, whilst there is a vegetarian fry-up
available in the morning of potato cakes with fresh herbs, scrambled
eggs, mushrooms and tomatoes, there is also the more traditional
Irish breakfast with its bacon and pudding.

What counts in Knockalla, however, aside from the wit of the owners
(their little card, with a drawing of the house on standard grey paper,
announces at the bottom: '100 per cent recycled, naturally') is the quality
of the ingredients used: eggs from their own flock of chickens, fresh herbs
plucked from the garden, their own organically grown produce and fresh
bread made with yeast and soda. In the evening, at dinnertime, this happy
transport of tastes is in full play: a summer tomato soup; leek stuffed
pancakes in a cheese sauce; baked stuffed marrow with potatoes,
beetrot and runner beans; lemon soaked sponge; chocolate mousse.

Fanad is one of the most alluringly seductive of the Donegal
peninsulas, and touring it offers endless delights and diversions and
also, in late autumn and throughout winter, a wind so lazy that rather
than wafting around you as you walk on the beaches, it just piles
straight through into your bones.

Open Mar-Nov
7 rooms, 3 en suite
Average Price: £12-£14
No Extra Charges
No Credit Cards
Dinner for guests £10, book by noon
No Licence (bring your own)
No Wheelchair Access
Children — high chairs, cots, babysitting
Recommended for Vegetarians
Pets accommodated
Enclosed Car Park
Just past Kerrykeel on the Ramelton/Portsalon road.

Town House

ANGLESEA TOWN HOUSE

63 Anglesea Road, Ballsbridge, Dublin 4 Tel: (01) 668 3877 Fax: 668 3461
Sean and Helen Kirrane

Anglesea feels like a private house, unlike others of the larger
Ballsbridge houses which cooly cater for business types and other
travellers who can't face a night in an hotel. This can mean that some
find it a little fussy, but that is a happy price to pay for such pleasureful
informality and spontaneity, for such a keen personal touch.

Like the best type of private house, the breakfasts in Sean and Helen
Kirrane's place just go on and on, and on and on. And then on and on
some more. Compote of fruits. Devilled kidneys. Kedgeree. Cereals.
Everything under the sun which can be included in a fried breakfast.
Fish. Yogurts. Coffees. Teas. On and on it goes, and on and on goes
your happy appetite along with it.

This early morning feast, all of it competently and charmingly served,
all of it setting you to rights before a strenuous day of working or
exploring, may be the last thing you enjoy in Ireland before setting off
for the boat and a return to Blighty, or it may be the first serious meal
you encounter after arriving in town late the previous night. The Town
House's location is perfect for arrivals and departures from either Dun
Laoghaire or the North Wall terminal.

Open all year except Xmas
7 rooms, all en suite
Average Price: £40 per person sharing
10% Service Charge
Credit Cards: Visa, Access
No Restaurant
No Licence
No Wheelchair Access
Children — welcome
Vegetarian breakfasts always offered
Pets allowed (not in rooms, garden at the back of the house)
Enclosed car park
Anglesea Road runs between Ballsbridge and Donnybrook.

Hostel
AVALON HOUSE
55 Aungier Street, Dublin 2 Tel: (01) 475 0001 Fax: 475 0303
Tom Kennedy

A modern hostel in an old, renovated building a stone's throw from St. Stephen's Green, Avalon is a testament to good planning, intelligent design and efficacious efficiency. There are nifty family rooms for nifty families — some of them en suite, but some of them rather lacking in curtains, it must be said. There is the occasional single room, and lots of double rooms, all of them with tamper-proof safety doors. For those travelling on the seat of their financial trousers there are nice small dorms at super-cheap prices.

All are bright, clean, and many of them have thoughtfully designed mezzanines which allow for extra privacy. Secure car parking can be arranged for a few quid per night, bikes can be locked up safely, and nightwatchmen make sure that the boisterous respect others' need for some shut-eye.

It is in the details of things such as showers and loos, usually the bug bears of places which accommodate scores of backpackers and others, that Avalon stands out, and which make it a place suitable for those who want simplicity and unfussiness and not just those travelling with a posse of kids who must watch the way the money goes. Showers give lots of private space, and blasts of hot water, loos are shared by the sexes and are cleverly designed to be cleaned and sorted out efficiently. Indeed, a premium is placed on cleanliness and hygiene right throughout the building.

In the public rooms downstairs the accent is again on amenable efficiency. A noticeboard tells you everything you might need to know about the city and its whys and ways. At breakfast there is real coffee, fresh rolls and orange juice. If you and your mates want to strum some guitars there is session space down in the basement, near the self-catering kitchens, from where no one else will hear you. And, all the while, the choicest sights of Dublin are within walking distance.

Open all year (including Xmas)
180 beds, divided into dorms, family rooms and doubles
Average Price: £7.50 dorm, from £11 per person twin, from £14 single
Breakfast £2.25-£3 Prices for rooms include linen
Credit Cards: Visa, Access/Master, Amex, Diners
Self-catering kitchen available
No Licence
Wheelchair Access (twin disabled room)
Children — welcome (family rooms)
Vegetarian breakfast offered
No pets
No car park (discount prices on nearby car park)
Aungier Street runs between Great George's Street and Wexford Street.

Guesthouse
AVONDALE HOUSE
Scribblestown, Castleknock, Co Dublin Tel: (01) 838 6545 Fax: 453 9099
Frank and Josie Carroll

Listening to the tales of people who have stayed in Avondale is akin to
meeting members of an obscure religious sect. They talk far, far too
quickly, in excited voices, as they describe their experiences in this
lovely house, they have the blazing eyes of converts smitten with the
one true faith, and can barely contain themselves within the framework
of conventional vocabulary.

There are only a pair of double and one single single room in Avondale,
not a lot with which to win such a cult reputation, not a lot with which
to begin a church of followers. But this trio of rooms have a cultness
born from the fact that many people are so charmed by their eccentric
lavishness, their interplay of Gothic with Ancient Greek, the ironic
alongside the ecclesiastical, the humorous with the how-de-do. The
intelligent eye behind all this work means, however, that the house
never trades in comfort for quirkiness: this is a comfortable, very
relaxing place.

As Dublin airport and the North Wall ferry terminal are just down the
road, Avondale is an excellent choice as a first-or-last nighter for those
who want to be proximate to the buzz of the capital, but don't want a
city location. Josie Carroll's cooking is good and good and simple, a
vital bonus for those who don't wish to hack into town to a restaurant.
And when you do get home, just remember to take a deep breath before
you start to describe the house to your friends. Otherwise, you will
sound like all those other converts, those apostles of Avondale.

Open 3 Jan-15 Dec
2 rooms, both en suite
Average Price: £32 per person sharing, £12 single supplement
No Extra Charges
No Credit Cards
Dinner for guests, book by noon, £18
Wine Licence
No Wheelchair Access
Children — cot available
Vegetarian meals available on request (please give notice)
Pets accommodated, but not in bedrooms
Safe Parking
Turn off the N3 at the Halfway House Pub, at the roundabout.

Guesthouse
CHESTNUT LODGE ➡
2 Vesey Place, Monkstown, Co Dublin Tel: (01) 280 7860
Nancy Malone

This beautiful, high-ceilinged Georgian house, rich with the folds of history, enjoys a marvellous location in the quiet embrace of a quiet Monkstown road, near to the ferry at Dun Laoghaire, close to town but far enough away to give one a flavour of the villages of Dublin. If its aspect is just right, it is further congratulated in the attention to small details which Nancy Malone ensures are in place in Chestnut: fine silver teapots, nutty soda bread and fresh orange juice at breakfast, delicious compotes and muesli which are one of Ms Malone's specialities —'Oh, when the strawberries are in season, my muesli is delicious!', she says, correctly — fine linen napery. The fact that such care is taken over every thing gives great pleasure, great reassurance. After a hard days' work in the big smoke, this is a lovely place to repair to for quiet, calmness. If you are just off the boat and beginning a holiday, then there is no better place to collect yourself and to begin to acquire those grace notes of the Irish holiday: hospitality, charm, true friendliness. 'Nancy and her daughters were charming, and next time we will certainly stay there', writes a correspondent from England, just returned home and still dreaming of the delight of it all.

Open all year
5 rooms,4 en suite
Average Price: £22.50-£27.50 per person sharing, £27.50-£37.50 single
No Extra Charges
Credit Cards: Visa, Access
Dinner on special request
No Licence (bring your own)
No Wheelchair Access
Children — welcome
Recommended for Vegetarians
No pets
No car park
Coming from Dublin direction, pass Monkstown Church, take the next turn right onto Sloperton Road.

Hotel
LONGFIELD'S HOTEL
Lwr Fitzwilliam Street, Dublin 2 Tel: (01) 676 1060 Fax: 676 1542
David Butt

This little hotel, smack in the centre of the city, has a very human face, and very tangible comforts which come from personal, attentive concern. Other hotels in Dublin may enjoy slightly better locations, they may have amassed grander reputations over the years, but it is to Longfield's that the smart money makes its way when it is in town. Where so many other hotels — indeed almost all other hotels — are now part of a chain or a group or a conglomerate or whathaveyou, Longfield's is individualistic, is calm and private and personable, and they try harder and work harder to maintain the standards they have set themselves. The food in Number 10, their basement restaurant, is excellent all the way from breakfast to supper, the location is perfect, and this is an ideal base whether your concerns are business or the more onerous business of pleasure.

Open all year except Xmas week
26 rooms, all en suite
Average Price: £80-£106 per person sharing, £60-£89.50 single
No Extra Charges
Credit Cards: Visa, Access/Master, Amex, Diners
Restaurant open for breakfast, lunch £12-£18, dinner £17.50-£21.95
Full Licence
Wheelchair Access
Children — welcome
Vegetarian dishes always available
No pets
No car park
Lwr Fitzwilliam Street runs between Baggot Street and Merrion Square.

Townhouse
NUMBER 31 ➡ £
31 Leeson Close, Dublin 2 Tel: (01) 676 5011 Fax: 676 2929
Brian and Mary Bennett

Like the memory of James Joyce's Ulyssean footsteps, or the crackle
and fizz of Roddy Doyle's Barrytown stories, Number 31 is now a part
of the city that is so familiar, so implicit, that you wonder how you
survived before it came along, offering the sweetest collusion of
avant garde architecture and old fashioned hospitality you can find.
The location of Brian and Mary Bennett's house, in a quiet mews
just off the strip of Leeson Street, means that the entire city is within
walking distance, with all the theatres, restaurants, shops and cinemas
no more than a healthifying jaunt away. This also means that visitors
feel they are truly in the city: Dublin is a city which makes more sense
when seen on foot than by any other way, for then one appreciates
the scale of this small and, in some places, perfectly formed place.
Number 31 itself is one of those places whose reputation has spread
at the pace of a bush fire: the same people keep coming back here,
followed quickly by the droves of friends to whom they have
recommended — indeed, probably insisted — that this is where
you stay when you stay in Dublin.
One will hear praise for the breakfasts, from starred chefs; praise for
the style of the house, from much-travelled journalists; praise galore,
from holidaymakers who discover this little miracle of modernist
design. The character of the house is distinctly Dublinesque: somewhat
knowing, slightly naïve, making things up as it goes along. One can
only add that booking Number 31 well in advance is essential, when
booking a trip to the capital.

Open all year except Xmas
4 en suite rooms, 1 with sauna
Average Price: from £29 per person sharing, £40 single
No Extra Charges
Credit Cards: Visa, Access/Master
No Restaurant facilities
No Licence
Wheelchair Access (possible with assistance, room on ground floor)
Children — over 12 only
Vegetarian breakfast available
No pets
Secure car park
Leeson Close runs off Lower Leeson Street.

B&B with Restaurant

CLIFF HOUSE

The Scrigeen, Kilronan, Aran Islands, Co Galway Tel: (099) 61286
Olwin & Michael Gill

Olwin Gill's cooking is generous and taste-loaded, able to offer
moments of quiet magic as you savour some roasted lamb and a plate
of floury spuds, a fresh grilled fillet of sole in a grainy mustard sauce,
an absurdly creamy strawberry-layered concoction for dessert. The
tastes are true and appropriate, perfect pleasure after a day in the
wind-blown wonder of Aran. The bedrooms in the B&B are simple
and fine value.

Whilst the simplicity and functionalism of Cliff House may not
suit those who hanker after cushy bourgeois bliss or pampered
pampootiedom, Olwin and Michael Gill's modest house is affordably
suitable, eminently suitable, when on Aran.

You can gaze through the big picture window, down onto the bobbing
bay of Kilronan, on a bright summer morning as you dissect an expert
breakfast. You can gaze down onto a more pacific bay at evening time,
waiting for an expert dinner to begin. Its location, snuck half a mile out
of Kilronan, means that it is always quiet and peaceable, allowing you
to snoringly ignore the revels of the village on summer weekend nights,
and affording access to some of the best walks along the western edge
of the island.

Open all year except Xmas
6 rooms, 2 en suite, 2 separate bathrooms
Average Price: £14 per person sharing, £16 en suite, £16 single
No Extra Charges
No Credit Cards
Restaurant open for dinner £13, booking essential
Wine Licence
No Wheelchair Access
Children — high chairs, cots, babysitting
Vegetarian meals with prior notice
No pets
Bicycle hire and minibus transport arranged
Take the boat from Rossaveal or Galway, or the 'plane from Galway.
Cliff House overlooks the harbour at Kilronan.

Hostel
MAINISTIR HOUSE ➡

Inis Mór, Aran Islands, Co Galway Tel: (099) 61169 Fax: 61351
Joël d'Anjou, Mairtin Mullen, Tara Rafferty

Mainistir House has always been a visionary venture, the pursuit of an ideal vision of hospitality and informality, of simplicity and satisfaction, culture and comfort. It is very much the vision of Joël d'Anjou, assisted perfectly by his trusty sidekicks Tara Rafferty and Mairtin Mullen, and it is true to say that no one else could make it succeed.

M d'Anjou makes it work by being a cultured man without a trace of snobbery, by being a private person who loves to share his space with people, by being of such a singular frame of mind that the idea of Mainistir — it is called a hostel but is closer to a pensione in design and orientation — offering accommodation to both backpackers and families, offering sublime food at a knockdown price in the format of a buffet in the evenings, offering at times what seems the essence of Aranness, is an ideal made real.

There is nowhere else like it, right from the sound of Gregorian chant on the tape player that begins the day, devolving later on into some Mozart arias, perhaps a little Miles Davis, or Willard White singing spirituals, all of them setting the mood and tone with judicious tempos. The 'Vaguely Vegetarian' buffets which Joël and Tara cook for dinner are happy, intelligent creations: a celery broth, some sweet grains and pulses, maybe even crab quiche, whatever takes their fancy on the day makes its way out to the dining room on top of great big North African plates. In summertime, Mainistir is perfect. For a unique Christmas, it is extraordinary. At any time, you will wish to be nowhere else but here.

Open all Year, including Christmas and New Year
Accommodated in twin rooms, double rooms, dorms, none en suite
Average Price: £7 per person (dorm), £12.50 per person (twin/double room)
No Service Charge. Laundry service £3 per load
Credit Cards: Visa, Access/Master
Dinner at 7pm winter, 8pm summer, reservation essential
No Licence (bring your own wine)
No Wheelchair Access
Children — welcome
Recommended for Vegetarians and Celiacs
When you arrive at the pier ask for Mairtin. He will drive you to the hostel.

B&B
ST. CIARAN'S ➡

Oughill, Inis Mór, Aran Islands, Co Galway Tel: (099) 61238
Bernadette Street

Bernadette and Jim Street's house, about a mile up the road from
Kilronan, is a house filled with discerning objects, cultured things,
items of craft that give pleasure when you see them first, but give
more pleasure when you look at them again. Then, one sees the happy
interplay of contrasts, between beautiful hand-stitched quilts which
line the walls and the fresh flowers on the tables, between the
effortlessly arranged items of sculpture that mingle glass with wood
or natural materials with man-made and the delicate functionalism
of fires and chests and chairs.

It's a bright, amusing house, with a lovely dining room in which
to enjoy your lovely breakfast, with so-cosy bedrooms, with arse-
swaggering ducks outside meandering amidst the squiggly geese
and the sleepy pooches.

You will fully need the bolstering charge of hearty porridge and some
fresh eggs, perhaps some apple and cinnamon or banana muffins with
a belt of strong tea, to persuade you to leave the house in the morning
and set about your explorations, for the temptation to simply stay and
loll contentedly is strong, so strong.

Open Mar-Oct
3 rooms sharing 1 shower room
Average Price: £15 per person sharing, £18 single
No Extra Charges
No Credit Cards
No restaurant, but tea, coffee, scones and muffins offered on arrival
No Licence
No Wheelchair Access
Children — high chairs, cots, babysitting
Recommended for Vegetarians
Pets accommodated, but not large dogs
Car Park not applicable
Take one of the mini buses from the pier, or the airport. There will be a small charge
but you'll find it's worth it.

B&B

RADHARC AN CHLAIR £

Inis Oirr, Aran Islands, Co Galway Tel: (099) 75019
Mrs Bríd Poíl

Arrive in the morning at Bríd Poíl's welcoming bungalow in the village of Baile an Chaisleáin, and the swaddling smell of just-baked bread might meet you, served with that cup of tea you need to revive the limbs after you have hauled your bags up from the boat or the 'plane. At dinner time you can expect the comforting odours of sweet lamb, just-right fish, the dry air of floury spuds, for Mrs Poíl is a fine cook. An enlivening appreciation and respect for food animates her work, all the way from soft, babbly soups to soporific, creamy cakes. Combined with excellent housekeeping and nonchalant comfort, it adds up to the ideal B&B. There is no better base from which to seek out the measure of little Inis Oirr, with its somewhat light-hearted soul, than this somewhat lighthearted B&B.

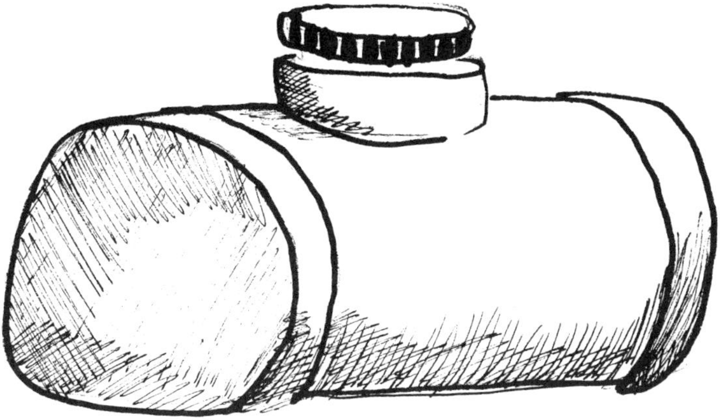

Open 1 Feb-30 Nov
6 rooms, 2 en suite, 4 sharing bathroom, shower room and extra toilet
Average Price: £11.50-£13 per person sharing, £15 single
No Extra Charges
No Credit Cards
Dinner for guests, £9.50
No Licence (bring your own)
No Wheelchair Access
Children — high chairs, cots, babysitting
Vegetarian meals always available
No pets
No Cars
Ask at the pier or the airport for directions, but Mr Poil collects people on the tractor when they know they are coming.

B&B
THE ANGLER'S RETURN
Toombeola, Roundstone, Co Galway Tel: (095) 31091
Lynn Hill

You don't need a full length Barbour and an Ena Sharples' hairnet to stay here, despite the name of this 18th century sporting lodge. The Angler's Return, once part of the Ballynahinch estate, enjoys a superb location for exploring this most indomitable, mysterious part of Connemara: close to Roundstone, close to Clifden, a scoot away from Maam, adjacent to the severe waters of Leenane. Even the spunky pubs of Galway are not too far away.

The house is a quiet, peaceably run and simply furnished in muted pastels that show some happy signs of maturity. The beds are high and soft, the rooms are places in which to sleep deeply. After a few days of driving and walking, hiking and scaling, sheltering from the rain and basking in the sunshine, that most entranced of epithets: 'I think this is the most beautiful part of the country', spills from your lips without even thinking. Maybe it is. Maybe it isn't. And, maybe, if you haven't been here yet, you have some idea of what you are missing.

Open May-end Oct (out of season by arrangement)
5 rooms, sharing 1 bathroom and 1 shower room
Average Price: £18-£20
No Extra Charges
No Credit Cards
Will book local restaurant with notice
No Licence
No Wheelchair Access
Children — welcome by arrangement
Recommended for Vegetarians
No pets
Enclosed car park
No business facilities
4 miles down the Ballynahinch-Roundstone road (leading off the main Galway-Clifden road)

Hotel
THE ARDAGH HOTEL
Ballyconneely Road Tel: (095) 21384 Fax: (095) 21314
Stephane Bauvet

So many times in Ireland, when you look at what might be described as a 'quiet, family hotel' overlooking a bay and think of the potential for perfection which the location offers, your heart sinks, rather than soars, because you know that, despite the beauty of the building and its picturesque surroundings, and with all the good intentions of the owners and staff, that the food will, most likely, be sloppy and the rooms, most likely, will be tawdry. You will rarely be able to rely on genuinely thoughtful service, or well considered, welcoming food, and a high standard of housekeeping in the rooms upstairs.
Stephane and Monique Bauvet's Ardagh Hotel is an exception to this rule, for this is a place you can rely on. The public rooms are comfortable, and so are the bedrooms, even if there is a slight sense of time-lag in their design. The cooking is of a uniformly high standard, and the staff are helpful and personable.
Food is available in the bar at lunchtime, and it will be good soups, open sandwiches which reveal the Dutch background of the owners, and oysters, to be eaten with cinnamon-tasting Guinness. The restaurant upstairs, which overlooks Ardbear Bay, is a wonderful site for Monique Bauvet's cooking, a blend of European influences with the best Irish ingredients: home marinated gravadlax, salad tiede with quail eggs and smoky bacon, black sole with a yellow and red sweet pepper sauce, Barbary duckling with caramelised apples and a Calvados sauce.

Open end Mar-Oct
21 rooms, all en suite
Average Price: from £31.50 per person sharing, £41.50 single
No Extra Charges
Credit Cards: Visa, Access/Master, Amex, Diners
Restaurant open, dinner £22
Full Pub Licence
No Wheelchair Access
Children — high chair, cot, family rooms
Vegetarian meals only with prior notice
Pets by arrangement only
Enclosed Car Park
The Ardagh is 2km outside Clifden on the road to Ballyconneely.

Hotel
BALLYNAHINCH CASTLE HOTEL
Recess, Connemara, Co Galway Tel: (095) 31006 Fax: 31085
John O'Connor

Though it is big beamed like a castle, and grey like an hotel,
Ballynahinch has never lost the principle of pleasure-pursuit which
led to its being built, originally, as a weekend sporting retreat.
Maharajah Ranjitsinji bought the house which is today Ballynahinch
Castle, back in the 1930s in order to entertain his friends during the
winter. Today, the Castle Hotel still feels more like a country house
than many of the country houses in Ireland. It is the air of unspoken
amiability which makes it so charming, and so unusual for an hotel.
It is relaxing and unpretentious, and staffed by young people who
disport themselves likewise.
Many come here to fish on the skirling river, others to shoot woodcock,
others for good-value winter weekends when big fires, agreeable food
and the do-nothing ambience of Ballynahinch find the place at its best.
The dining room is charming and romantic, the cooking is good without
ever perhaps achieving a measure of distinction. Those bedrooms which
face the river are well worth the extra money, as these offer the best
views and the most space. For walking, for losing yourself for a few
days, the surrounding countryside is heartbreakingly beautiful.

Open all year (including Xmas), except the month of Feb
28 rooms, all en suite
Average Price: high season £40-£60, low £38-£43, single supplement £17
No Extra Charges
Credit Cards: Visa, Access/Master, Amex, Diners
Restaurant open for dinner £23, pub lunch
Full Licence
No Wheelchair Access
Children — welcome
Vegetarian dishes always available
Pets, with prior notice
Enclosed car park
Signposted on the N71 road from Galway to Clifden.

Country House

CROCNARAW COUNTRY HOUSE

Moyard, Connemara, Co Galway Tel: (095) 41068
Lucy Fretwell

The laid-back lackadaisicality of Crocnaraw quite suits the understated ambience of Lucy Fretwell's country house. Inside, function triumphs over style in a strict 'no-contest', while the proportions of Crocnaraw and its soft colours and design eccentricities are pleasing.

With the easygoing evening time food to enjoy — baked eggs, roast lamb, fillets of brill, creamed spuds, nursery puds — the fine breakfasts, the modest prices and impeccable location for touring, Crocnaraw allows you to play to its strengths.

Open May-Oct
7 rooms, 5 en suite
Average Price: b&b per person sharing £21-£30
No Extra Charges
Credit Cards: Visa, Access
Restaurant open for dinner, 8pm, book by noon
Wine Licence
Wheelchair Access (1 room on ground floor)
Children — no facilities
Vegetarian meals available (give notice please)
Pets allowed
Enclosed car park
Six miles north of Clifden on the road to Westport.

Country House
CURRAREVAGH HOUSE
Oughterard, Connemara, Co Galway Tel: (091) 82312 Fax: 82731
Harry and June Hodgson

Devotees of Harry and June Hodgson's house are devoted to so many
things about it. They enjoy arriving at the modest entrance to the
house, enjoy entering into the timeworn style of the capacious hall,
with fishermen's well-worn wellies lined up, with the fireplace
flickering and the promise of the comfy facing chairs and, especially,
they like the lure of the quirky little bar which snuggles under the
wind of the staircase. Step in here, and you step back to the days of
De Valera and Clem Attlee, find yourself in Merchant-Ivory territory.
They like the gargantuan breakfasts, helping themselves to lashings of
fried eggs and mounds of June Hodgson's wonderful, simple kedgeree,
tilting the science-lab coffee percolators repeatedly into their cups.
They like the gong before dinner, then the procession into the dining
room as if this was Upper Table and they like, especially, the fact that
it is a distinctly 'jackets on for gentlemen' sort of scenario. Then, the
separate tables for each party, the solid food with its distinct nursery
echoes — duck liver pâté, trout with hollandaise, roast beef with
Yorkshire pud and horseradish, a bilberry brulée — and the bottles of
wine, originally opened last night, all set to be drained.
Later, there will maybe be a walk around the lip of glorious Lough Corrib,
or a tumble into the deep chairs in the drawing room, before bed. Things
in Currarevagh have changed little, and it is this lack of change, this
refusal to progress, which is what the devotees of Currarevagh like.
The house offers an archetypal vision of nostalgia, a place apart with
people all in their place, honey still for tea.

Open Easter-Oct
15 rooms, all en suite
Average Price: from £41 per person sharing, £56 single
10% service charge
No Credit Cards
Evening meal available, £18
Full Licence
No Wheelchair Access
Children — cot, high chair available
Vegetarian meals available only by prior arrangement
Pets by arrangement
Enclosed car park
Follow the 'Lakeshore' road out of Oughterard.

Self Catering Cottages
DELPHI COTTAGES
Leenane, Co Galway Tel: (095) 42213 Fax: 44212
Jane & Peter Mantle

The panoply of lakes, rivers and inlets which so confidently and
graciously surround the astute manor of Delphi, the pitching hills
and snaking roads around which you wend in open-jawed awe at the
turbulent beauty of the waters and the hills, makes this entire area
nothing less than the Dordogne of the west.

Here, nature is always serving up another super-duper sunset, lacing
the water's surface with ticker-tapes of scooting foam, blowing fresh
breezes to entice you out of the car and down to the water's edges, or
up across the moors and hills. It is an area prized by those patient
spirits who chase fish with colouful flies, but you don't need a
Barbour and wellies to bask in the ominous beauty of this haunch
of Connemara.

What you do need is a base from which to explore, and Delphi Lodge,
a restored sporting lodge has not only comfortable rooms within the
house, but bright and functional self-catering Cottages as well. Out of
season they can be rented for as little as three days at a time, and shared
between a quartet of travellers they are more than affordable. They are
modest in size, but furnishings are agreeable and the various necessaries
are thoughtfully provided. Dinner — served at a massive oak table —
can be taken in Delphi Lodge if you choose to make a reservation.

Open all year except 1 Nov-31 Jan
Each self-catering cottage sleeps 4. Weekly prices: low season £225, high £350; daily:
£40 low, £60 high (min stay three days). The main house has seven en suite bedrooms.
Prices are between £30 and £45 per person sharing, per night depending on season and
view (min stay two nights).
Extra Charges: Electricity in cottages
Credit Cards: Visa, Access
Dinner available in the main house, provided it's not fully booked by guests.
Wine Licence
No Wheelchair Access   No children in house unless fishing
Vegetarian dinner available on request
No pets   Car park
At Leenane turn right on the N59 (signpost Westport) and drive to the end of the
Lough. Turn left at the sign to Delphi. The estate is seven miles further on.

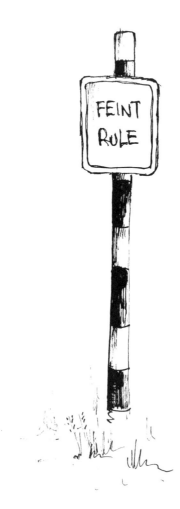

B&B
KILLE HOUSE
Kingstown, Clifden Tel: (095) 21849
Anya Brand Vermoolen

Kille is a house of sumptuous, pristine elegance. You would be happy
to be here regardless of whether the views were deathly dull or
breakfasts were boring, but the location of the house near to the Sky
road allows for vistas of endless fascination, and Anya not only gives
the house great good cheer, she is also a splendid cook.
She scrambles fresh eggs to a rich and velvety emulsion, makes a softly
toothsome meat loaf, offers splendid salamis, has an array of fine
cheeses, and there is crumbly, warm bread and excellent coffee.
The housekeeping is of such an extraordinary standard that there are
few other places in the country to which Kille can be compared, and
you fold yourself into a big, snowy-white duvet in a big beautiful bed in
a big handsome room, and thank the stars you are in Connemara, and
here in Kille.

Open 1 Apr-31 Oct
4 rooms, 2 en suite, 2 sharing 1 bathroom
Average Price: £17-£22 per person sharing, single supplement £5
No Extra Charges
No Credit Cards
Dinner for guests £15, book by noon
No Licence
No Wheelchair Access
Children — on request
Vegetarian meals always available
No pets
Enclosed Car Park
Ask directions for the Sky Road, and from this you will see the small hand-written sign
directing you to the house.

Country House
MOYCULLEN HOUSE

Moycullen, Co Galway Tel: (091) 85566
Philip & Marie Casburn

Moycullen is one of those houses that offers the peace of familiarity and the assurance of fond memories each and every time you return to it. Like a gin and tonic at six o'clock, or marmalade on your toast at breakfast, it is nothing new, but something you always want. Partly this is the house itself: an old sporting lodge built for wild west of Ireland weekends, it is unpretentious, cosy, an affable place. Architecturally it is a rarity in Ireland, set precisely in the Arts and Crafts style, a design which allows it to seem quaint yet proud, and which evokes visions of GBS in his tweeds, or Cary Grant in something smarter, sitting in the lounge reading yesterday's papers.

But it is Philip and Marie Casburn themselves who provide the core of Moycullen's soft focus, hazy and lazy air. Their easy ease, and Marie's unflustered comfort cooking, are as essential a part of Moycullen as the antique baths, the cushiony carpets, the cranky furniture, the buckets of fresh air.

Everything in the house, from the beds with their soft creakiness, to the gripping comfort of the chairs, to the succulence of mashed spuds with roast lamb preceded by kidneys in a sherry sauce and followed by a big creamy gateau, seems to knock the pent-up stuffing out of you, leaving you wanting more of this restfulness, and more of this graceful, naïve, house.

Open beginning Mar-end Nov
5 double bedrooms, each with private bath
Average Price: £25 per person sharing, £35 single
No Extra Charges
Credit Cards: Visa, Access
Dinner at 7pm, £17
No Licence (bring your own)
No Wheelchair Access
Children — welcome
Vegetarian meals available given notice
No pets
Car park
Moycullen House is off the N59. Turn left in Moycullen village, taking the Spiddal road and drive until you see the sign for the house.

Townhouse
NORMAN VILLA ★ £
86 Lwr Salthill, Galway Tel: (091) 21131
Dee and Mark Keogh

It has been fascinating, indeed it has been thrilling, to see how Mark
and Dee Keogh's beautiful house has begun, in the last couple of years,
to acquire a life all of its own.

Each time one returns, the changes, the improvements and the
simplifications which the Keoghs have made to the layout and the
design of this amusing and intelligent building seem always to have
gifted the house with greater personality than before. Norman Villa
seems to have its own heartbeat, its own soul: first you say hello to
Mark and Dee, then you say hello to Norman. 'Nice to see you again.
How have you been? Changed a little here and there. I like it, I like it'.
People may look at you just the way they looked at James Stewart
when he talked to Harvey the giant white rabbit. Pay no attention
to them.

This is an exquisite house, distinguished by the purity, utility and
finesse of its design and furnishings. The Keoghs feed its needs by
constant re-invention, constant enquiry as to how the house can be
improved. Last time you were here, you reckoned it was perfect. Yet,
this time, it's even better. It's a house which is worthy of 'The World of
Interiors', except that the bright and busy characters of Mark and Dee
give Norman a living, pulsing character: this is a fun house, and its
beauty is here to be enjoyed, not just admired. There is great
appreciation of materials: the prim play between brass beds and linen
sheets, between varnished floor boards and working window shutters,
between covetable art and quiescent coloured walls.

Breakfasts are terrific, and in terms of value for money, Norman has
few peers in Ireland.

Open all year except 10-31 Jan
5 rooms, 2 en suite
Average Price: b&b per person sharing, en suite £17, other £15, single en suite £22,
otherwise £20
£2 extra on certain weekends, eg Xmas and Racing
No Credit Cards
Dinner by special arrangement, open for Xmas dinner
No Licence   No Wheelchair Access
Children — £11.25 for under 12yrs
Vegetarian breakfasts available
No pets
Enclosed car park
One mile from city centre, follow signs for Lower Salthill, the house is 500 yards from
Claddagh Palace Cinema.

B&B
ROSE COTTAGE
Rockfield, Moyard, Co Galway Tel: (095) 41082
The Shanley-O'Toole family

If you want to get drunk in Clifden, haul yourself penitentially up
Croagh Patrick — it's not really that difficult, though the calf muscles
do sting for about a week after you have made it to the top — or plot a
route around the Twelve Bens and get lost in this exhaustedly daring
countryside, then Rose Cottage is the sort of place that won't get in
your way while you are at it.

Whilst it is something of an unexceptionable place — a modern
dormer bungalow with efficient rather than characterful bedrooms
and interlacing dining rooms downstairs which cater for droves of
travellers during the season — a combination of an unbeatable location
and keen prices, not to mention a dolorous charm and relaxed good
nature from the young women who scuttle busily around at breakfast
time, adds up to a good base for exploring Connemara.

Open May-Sept
6 rooms, all en suite
Average Price: £15 per person
No Extra Charges
No Credit Cards
Dinner available for guests, book by 3pm, £13.50
Wine Licence
No Wheelchair Access
Children — welcome
Vegetarian meals available (please give notice)
No pets
Enclosed car park
Rose Cottage is six miles north of Clifden.

Country House
ROSLEAGUE MANOR
Letterfrack, Connemara, Co Galway Tel: (095) 41101 Fax: 41168
Anne Foyle

Rosleague is a therapeutic place. Look out from the bedrooms at the front of the house and the view across Diamond Hill, Letter Hill and Speckled Hill, framed by the inrush of Ballynakill Harbour, is a tonic of pure, devoted wilderness and wildness.

The calm concord of the public rooms and the elegant conservatory pitch the body into baleful relaxation, whether you enjoy a simple lunch at the bar, or repair to them after dinner in order to rest up before resting up.

The cooking, now under the guidance of Nigel Rush, remains considerate and impressive, for even though Paddy Foyle has begun to concentrate his energies in Clifden, he has installed a happy team who continue to work under his direction, and the dining room is one of the most beautiful in the country, a commodious space where kids in their pyjamas don't feel discouraged from entering to steal a final goodnight kiss.

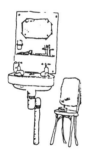

Open Easter to Nov
20 rooms (incl 4 mini suites) all en suite
Average Price: low season £45-£55, high £55-£70 per person
No Extra Charges
Credit Cards: Visa, Access/Master, Amex
Dinner, 8pm-9pm, £24
Full Pub Licence
No Wheelchair Access
Children — welcome
Vegetarian meals on request
Pets by arrangement, but not in public rooms
Car park available
The house is signposted from Letterfrack.

Guesthouse
SCREEBE HOUSE

Camus, Connemara, Co Galway Tel: (091) 74180
Nikolai Burkart

Just south of the great mountainy molars of Maam Valley,
Screebe House is a centenarian sporting lodge, snuggled between the
mountains and the winsome stretch of Camus Bay over which it holds
sole fishing rights.

Rooms are large and colourful, furnishings are intriguing, with en suite
bathrooms occupying their own space and involving intriguingly
complex, Heath Robinsonish plumbing. Views from the front of the
house glide over bunny-strewn gardens, whilst the rooms at the back
of the house have even more splendid — panoramic — vistas of what
is, surprisingly, tidal sea water, but which looks to the untrained eye
as a slightly flustered stretch of lakeland.

Service can be brazenly blasé, on occasion, but occasional foibles can
be forgotten as you enter the spirit of adventure of Screebe, and enjoy
the excellent cooking and the superb location.

Open Mar-Nov (out of season by arrangement)
6 rooms, all en suite
Average Price: £30 per person sharing
12.5% Service Charge
Credit Cards: Visa, Access
Restaurant serves lunch £10, dinner £20
Full Licence
No Wheelchair Access
Children — welcome
Vegetarian meals available (give notice when booking)
No pets
Car park
Signposted from Maam Cross.

Self-Catering Cottages
WALL'S FARM
Rinnaknock, Headford, Co Galway Tel: (093) 35661
Zara Brady

As well as breeding pedigree goats on the family farm, just by the
shores of Lough Corrib, Zara Brady organises the maintenance of
her self-catering cottage with relentless energy: last year it was an
all-weather tennis court which was finally completed, to the delight
of guests. This year will see a full size croquet court in operation.
The cottage sleeps approximately 5 people, depending on how well
you know each other, or how well you wish to get to know each other.
There is one double bedroom with en suite bathroom, two single
rooms, again with their own bathroom, and a small bunk room. For
families, this is an ideal place: there are ponies to ride and boats to
mess about in, and parents can relax whilst youngsters raise hell all on
their own in perfect safety. Unlike modern resorts, which occupy kids
at enormous and constant financial cost to their folks, Wall's Farm
allows the kids a true taste of the country and doesn't break the bank.
Buying the vegetables, eggs and milk direct from the farm is especially
rewarding because there is a very well equipped kitchen in which to
turn memorable ingredients into memorable meals, to be enjoyed
outside on the fifty-foot-long flower-decked sun terrace, or, on winter
days, in the dining room. There will be tears from those young ones
when it is time to go home, won't there?

Open all year round
Self-catering cottage to sleep 5
Average Prices: low season £200 per week, mid-season £250-£350, high season £400
Extra Charges: electricity, approx £10 per week
No Credit Cards
Organic vegetables and herbs, free-range eggs, goat's milk and ready-cooked meals
for sale
No Licence
No Wheelchair Access
Children — welcome
Recommended for Vegetarians
Pets allowed if kept under control
Enclosed car park
6 miles due west of Headford, on the shores of Lough Corrib.

Restaurant with Rooms
THE QUAY HOUSE
Clifden Tel: (095) 21369
Paddy Foyle

The Quay House, in a glorious location right on the waterfront in
Clifden, is the latest stage of Paddy Foyle's clever re-invention of his
métier. Like the last stage, the wonderful Destry Rides Again restaurant
just up the road in the town, Dermot Gannon will again be rattling the
pots and pans in the kitchen.
The mere association of any venture with the person of Mr Foyle is as
close to a guarantee of success as you can get, for he brings a stylishness
and understated confidence to each venture. The Quay House is going
to be a very hot ticket indeed.

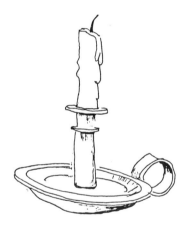

Open all year except Xmas and Jan
6 rooms, all en suite
Average Price: £25-£40 per person
No Extra Charges
Credit Cards: Visa, Access/Master
Dinner from £10
Wine Licence
Wheelchair Access
Children — welcome
Vegetarian meals by arrangement
No pets in bedrooms
Street Parking
On the seafront at Clifden.

Restaurant with Rooms
D'ARCY'S OLD BANK HOUSE
Main Street, Kenmare, Co Kerry Tel & Fax: (064) 41589
Matt & Aileen d'Arcy

The Old Bank House, right at the top of Kenmare's bright, wide Main Street, is a simple collection of rooms: affordable, so you can spend more money on Matt d'Arcy's fine food; informal, but with the necessary bits and pieces to put you at your ease in this most easeful town.
Mr d'Arcy has been best known over the last years as the head chef in the illustrious Park Hotel, and indeed his calling is very much that of the chef rather than the people-handler: he is a kitchen person, which lets you get on with looking after yourself while he gets on with the business of lunch and dinner.
His new premises may be much simpler than the grandeur of The Park, but the strengths of d'Arcy's cooking — strong flavours, impressive technical command of his craft and a flair for complicating and combining — are every bit as evident here as before, producing very classic and yet very modern food, the product of a long apprenticeship and a lot of learning. In the modest dining room, in the company of a good bottle from the wine list, it is fun to enjoy it all.

Open all year except 25-26 Dec (weekends only off season)
5 rooms, 2 en suite (3 share 1 bathroom)
Average Price: from £12.50-£15 per person
No Extra Charges (rooms £2 cheaper if you wish to skip breakfast)
Credit Cards: Visa, Access
Restaurant open 6pm-11pm, £15-£20
Wine Licence
No Wheelchair Access
Children — welcome
Vegetarian food always available
Pets allowed
In the centre of Kenmare town, at the top end of Main Street.

Townhouse
DOYLE'S TOWNHOUSE
John Street, Dingle, Co Kerry Tel: (066) 51174
John & Stella Doyle

John and Stella Doyle's restaurant has an international reputation, so it may come as a surprise to those who visit for the first time to see just what an informal place Doyle's Seafood Restaurant actually is: flagged floors, back-to-the-wall seating, an easily understated décor and an absence of any fussiness in either the food or the service, the perfect surroundings for a pint of stout and some shellfish. In this dining room the strengths of Doyle's — good bread, good house wines by the half-litre jug, efficiency — seem perfectly appropriate.

This functionalism is counterpointed by the fine, svelte good taste of the six rooms in Doyle's Townhouse, which adjoins the restaurant. The rooms have the confidence of good taste, with well-chosen, clever, useful design, the touch of something done well, done just right, and a comfortable night will be happily rounded off by a fine breakfast in which the delicious homemade sausages pair off with some heavenly black pudding.

Open mid Mar-mid Nov
8 rooms, all en suite
Average Price: £31 per person sharing, £39 single
No Extra Charges
Credit Cards: Visa, Access/Master, Diners
Restaurant open for dinner, from £13.50
Full Licence
No Wheelchair Access
Children — welcome
Vegetarian meals with 24 hours notice
No pets
Street Parking
In Dingle town centre.

B&B

HAWTHORN HOUSE

Shelbourne Street, Kenmare, Co Kerry Tel: (064) 41035
Kevin and Trina Murphy.

They are a good pair, Kevin and Trina, a good team, a Tracy and
Hepburn of the B&B business, with a Bogie and Bacall unity and
confluence which makes their hard work appear almost effortless,
their fastidiousness seem instinctive.

Hawthorn is a sweet and charming house, a paragon of hospitality
and housekeeping, with every detail attended to in order to ensure that
things are just so, just right. It is truly one of those places you want to
find yourself in when on holiday in the laid-back yet eager town of
Kenmare: friendly, genuine, honest-to-goodness.

Open all year, except Xmas
8 rooms, all en suite
Average Price: £18-£22 per person sharing, £19 single
No Extra Charges
Credit Cards: Visa, Access
No restaurant
Wine Licence
No Wheelchair Access
Children — cot available
Vegetarian food served
No pets
Enclosed car park
In the centre of Kenmare at the top of the hill.

B&B
THE OLD STONE HOUSE
Cliddaun, Dingle, Co Kerry Tel & Fax: (066) 59882
Michael & Becky O'Connor

This is just the kind of place you want to find when touring the exotic
and uncontainable delights of County Kerry, just the kind of retreat
you want thanks to being close to a buzzy place like Dingle, but far
enough away to allow you to escape into the quietude of the country.
Michael and Becky O'Connor's house is cosy, small — there are only
three bedrooms — and satisfyingly intimate, and the family are an
unquenchable fount of information and an inexhaustible source of
organisation pertaining to everything which the traveller may want to
do when in this melodiously lovely part of Kerry. Whether your aim
and intention is archaeology or Zen meditation, they will know how
to set you on the right track to finding exactly what you want.
The County of Kerry can seem an almost unknowable place,
dotted with friendly villages and towns but still someplace where the
countryside, with its wild and mischievous character, takes pride of
place. It can be possible to look down valleys and across the hills and
to see three entirely different vistas simultaneously within an eyesight,
possible to think you have the measure of the place, only to realise
that there are as many other aspects left unknown as you have come
to understand.

Open all year, including Xmas
3 bedrooms
Average Price: £15 per person sharing, £20 single
No Extra Charges
Credit Cards: Visa, Access
No Restaurant
No Licence
No Wheelchair Access
Children — welcome
Vegetarian breakfast always available
No pets
Enclosed car park
2.5 miles from Dingle town on the main road to Ventry.

Hotel
THE PARK HOTEL KENMARE ★
Kenmare, Co Kerry Tel: (064) 41200 Fax: 41402
Francis Brennan

Grandness, glamour, graciousness: if there is an ideal in all our minds of just what a great hotel should offer, then it is likely that Francis Brennan's Park Hotel will not only contain all these key notes — a sense of timelessness, a sense of idyll — but that it will, furthermore, add to them an unrelentingly true sense of hospitality. Mr Brennan is, quite simply, the very personification, the very essence, of the hotelier. His skills are so effortless and so graceful that you can't imagine that he ever actually learnt them. Far more likely, you reckon, that he was born this way, popped from the womb with this integral and instinctive grasp of how to run an hotel to the very highest standards, and then some.

Where most of those places which number themselves amongst the great hotels of the world operate by means of a system of formality and efficiency, rather than personal contact, the Park, whilst being thunderously efficient, of course, enjoys an affability and spontaneity amongst the staff which adds that essential human spark, without which all the rest would be meaningless.

So, The Park is grand, but extremely relaxed and comfortable. It is old, but has all manner of modern gee-gaws for those who must remain fixated by the phone or fax. It is a good place to use as a base, or you can stay here and eat here and do nothing more than stroll around Kenmare village to your heart's content. It is expensive, but seems very good value.

Above all, it is civilised, and civilising. It operates according to an ideal, that same ideal we all of us have in our mind about what a great hotel should be, and it strives at every second to live up to that ideal.

Open 2 Jan-15 Apr, mid Nov-23 Dec
50 rooms, all en suite
Average Price: from £92 per person sharing, £128 single
No Extra Charges
Credit Cards: Visa, Access/Master, Amex, Diners
Restaurant open for dinner, £36, booking essential
Full Bar Licence
Wheelchair Access
Children — no children under 5 yrs
Vegetarian meals with prior notice
No pets
Private Car Park
The gates to the Park are at the top of the hill in Kenmare town centre.

Restaurant with Rooms
TONLEGEE HOUSE
Athy, Co Kildare Tel: (0507) 31473
Mark and Marjorie Molloy

'I should like particularly to congratulate the Molloys. Nothing was ever too much trouble, and the food was exceptional'. This remark in a letter from an English traveller who could declare that during their holiday in Ireland — with a couple of exceptions — 'everyone, everything and everywhere was magnificent', is the kind of talk-talk you hear about Mark and Marjorie Molloy's Tonlegee House.

Partly, this affection is built on the basis of Mark Molloy's cooking, an ambitious, charged cuisine which wraps itself up in culinary complexities — boudin of chicken with pistachio nuts and a Pommery mustard sauce, escalope of salmon with mussels and a fresh basil sauce, guinea fowl with roast garlic and a thyme flavoured jus, chocolate and almond flavoured marjolaine (this a dish in tribute to his wife, perhaps?) — but which is always capable of making flavours hit home, creating dishes that are often truly memorable.

But it is the atmosphere created by a young couple working hard in their own place and slowly improving it, slowly knocking it to rights, adding on a quintet of comfy rooms to truly turn it into a restaurant with rooms, it is this motivation which creates the energy and the thrill of Tonlegee, makes it a place where nothing is too much trouble.

Open all year except Xmas
5 rooms, all en suite
Average Price: per room £58 double
No Extra Charges
Credit Cards: Visa, Access/Master
Restaurant open Mon-Sat 7pm-9.30pm ('till 10.30pm Fri & Sat), £20
Full Licence
No Wheelchair Access
Children — high seats, cots
Vegetarian meals available (notice helps)
No Pets
Enclosed car park
In Athy, cross two bridges and take the Kilkenny road out of town. Very soon you will see their sign telling you to go left.

Guesthouse
BLANCHVILLE HOUSE
Dunbell, Maddoxtown, Co Kilkenny Tel: (056) 27197
Monica Phelan

As you drive up to Blanchville House and a crazy big granite
construction on the right hand side seizes your attention with its
surreal sense of stupidity, don't go thinking to yourself that some fool
built a tower but, somehow, forgot to append a respectable church
onto the back of it. There was never a church to begin with, just a bell
tower without bells, a clock tower without clocks. This is that rare
thing in Ireland: an architectural folly.

This is likely to be your last brush with folly, however, for Monica
Phelan runs an expert, feel-good organisation in Blanchville. You
meet your fellow residents in the drawing room before setting down to
dinner and these, eaten communally around a great big table, are fun
affairs — the cooking is good, the crack can be mighty as you speculate
on the affairs of Irish politicians, the affairs of English politicians and,
hell, the affairs of anyone else whom you and your fellow diners may
share as acquaintances.

The house runs on a fair degree of panicky energy but, even when
things get done a little bit late, they do get done right. The bedrooms
are quaintly welcoming and have all the magazines that always seem
much more interesting when they are in someone else's house.
Breakfasts, again communal, allow for another chance to pursue
further gossip, whilst snugly embedded in the bourgeois succulence
of a fine manor house.

Open 1 Mar-1 Nov
6 rooms, 4 en suite, 2 with private bath
Average Price: £23-£25 per person
No Extra Charges
Credit Cards: Visa, Access
Dinner 7.30pm-8pm £15, book by noon
No Licence (bring your own wine)
No Wheelchair Access
Children — welcome with advance notice
Vegetarian dishes available (give notice please)
Outside facilities for pets
Enclosed car park
5 miles from Kilkenny, off the N10 Dublin road.

Guesthouse
CULLINTRA HOUSE
The Rower, Inistioge, Co Kilkenny Tel: (051) 23614
Patricia Cantlon

Here is the sort of thing people write to you concerning Patricia
Cantlon's Cullintra House:
'Dear Mr and Mrs McKenna,
'A week ago we were in Ireland, staying at Cullintra House, and one
week on, the place is already becoming a legend amongst our friends.'
Not just 'celebrated', note: 'a legend', indeed, a legend and no less.
This is how Cullintra House enjoys the cult reputation which it does.
How a small country house can acquire a cult reputation is difficult
to understand, but most everyone seems to have heard of it and most
everyone seems to have an opinion about it, often regardless of whether
they have actually stayed there. It is, simply, that sort of place: easy to
gossip about, fun to gossip about. Some hate it and find its
eccentricities intolerable, for others these eccentricities are what makes
it a legend, as our correspondent noted: 'Cullintra suited us, and it is
certainly most unusual, though I can imagine a lot of people finding it
just too unorthodox. We didn't mind too much that the cows attempted
to demolish the car, and we have managed to straighten the spotlight
out now'. Well, orthodoxy never made anyone famous.
The legendary lateness of dinner may explain part of this reputation,
though in truth the lateness of dinner tends to get exaggerated. For the
devotees of Cullintra, evenings that tumble out into the small hours as
you chew over the reputations and morals of your mutual friends are
sheer bliss, with every evening a house party amongst yourself and
your new-found friends. Patricia's cooking consoles and comforts,
just what you wanted.
It is not strictly necessary to go to Cullintra to have an opinion about it
but it is most decidedly the best way to acquire an opinion about it.

Open all year (minimum two nights)
6 rooms incl. a family suite of 3 adjoining rooms and shower, and an open plan
apartment in outside hay barn (sleeps 2 couples who don't mind co-habiting a
smallish space)
Average Price: £18 per person sharing, £23 single
No Extra Charges   No Credit Cards
Patricia expects you to stay for dinner £14
No Licence (bring your own wine)
No Wheelchair Access
Children — welcome
Vegetarian meal available (must give prior notice)
No pets
Enclosed car park
6 miles from New Ross on the Kilkenny road.

Restaurant with Rooms
LACKEN HOUSE
Dublin Road, Kilkenny, Co Kilkenny Tel: (056) 61085 Fax: 62435
Eugene and Breda MacSweeney

The rooms in Lacken House are small, and perfectly formed: you
sleep here, sleep well, but you can hold neither convocation, sorority
seminar or ballroom dancing heat in the rooms. Their function is to
afford you rest after the less than arduous labour of eating one of
Eugene MacSweeney's delicious dinners and quaffing your way, with
the expert assistance of Breda MacSweeney, through the wine list.
With everything he cooks, Mr MacSweeney exploits the long-learnt
skill of the professional cook, but skill, here, is used to extract flavour,
to reveal the character and essence of a food. Mr MacSweeney never
shows off, never lets things get complicated just for the hell of it, just
because he can do it.
You will also find that the cooking shows someone who has never
lost touch with the scents, attractions and satisfactions of the garden
and the ground: he likes to spirit the green, wild tastes of herbs and
leaves such as nettles and parsley into dishes to offer a counterpoint
to the luxury of prime cuts and complex tastes. Involved food needs
simple, earthy tastes to make it both enjoyable and digestible, and
Mr MacSweeney knows this better than most cooks. You find the
true tastes of Irish food, and Irish hospitality, here in Lacken House,
in this lovely place in what may be the loveliest town in Ireland.

Open all year except Xmas week
8 rooms, all en suite
Average Price: £25 per person sharing, £31 single low season, £28 per person
sharing, £34 single high season
No Extra Charges
Credit Cards: Visa, Access/Master, Amex, Diners
Restaurant open Tue-Sat dinner £22
Full Restaurant Licence
No Wheelchair Access
Children — high chair, cots and babysitting with prior notice
Recommended for Vegetarians
No pets (except guide dogs)
Enclosed Car Park
Signposted on the Dublin Road just as you go into Kilkenny

Country House
ROUNDWOOD HOUSE
Mountrath, Co Laois Tel: (0502) 32120
Frank & Rosemary Kennan

Is there a benefit to being somewhere small, easily set to the back of the mind, to being as modest and unsung a place as County Laois is? Perhaps. What may be grandiose elsewhere, it seems, is unforced here, unassuming. A pub like Morrissey's in Abbeyleix, were one to transport it to Dublin or Galway, would quick become a pickled tourist trap, somewhere famous for being famous. In Abbeyleix, this extraordinary pub simply gets on with the business of serving drink, as it has done for decades, refusing to allow time to change it, still with a counter of foods, still with the old biscuit tins, still with the respect for a fine pint of stout which they have always pulled.

This modesty extends to Frank and Rosemary Kennan's Roundwood House, one of the most affectionately regarded places to stay in the entire country. An air of pleasure-filled idyll pervades, and you could almost believe it was the product of the air that sweeps down Slieve Bloom, such is the ease with which this house operates. Roundwood is so story-book super, with its commingling ducks and its horses, its wide rooms with tall windows, you might imagine yourself transported to some never-never land. Rosemary Kennan's cooking is expert, soulful, flavour-addled, full of intriguing twists which her hungry mind adds to the repertoire of country house fare which regulars demand. Breakfasts are scrumptious, and dinner a culinary delight of modest, skilful food. The visitors' book, almost more than any other in the entire country, pays tribute to the Kennans' skill, their concern, their quiet savoir faire. You too will be queueing up to trump up superlative notes of thanks.

Open all year except Xmas
6 rooms, all en suite
Average Price: £32 per person sharing, £38 single
No Extra Charges — 10% discount for 2 nights
Credit Cards: Visa, Access/Master, Amex, Diners
Dinner for guests and non residents £19, book by 4pm
Wine Licence
No Wheelchair Access
Children — high chairs, cots, babysitting
Varied Vegetarian options always available
Pets accommodated, but not in rooms
Private Car Parking
Roundwood House is signposted from Mountrath. If in dobt follow signs for Slieve Bloom.

Country House

BALLYTEIGUE HOUSE

Bruree, nr Charleville, Co Limerick Tel: (063) 90575
Margaret Johnson

You have just vaulted the Atlantic in a jet, picked up a hire car and
motored the sixty minutes from Shannon airport which it takes to get
to Ballyteigue House. You are sitting in the drawing room in front of a
hungry, bright fire and you cannot believe your luck. Already, you are
likely thinking in the sort of tones and terms which decorated an effusive
letter from a reader who stayed in Ballyteigue for no less than ten days:
'The service was impeccable and the personal touch of our welcoming
hostess was never missing. It was such a surprise to know that she even
cooked all the meals herself and what meals!!'
Not just one, but two exclamation marks. If this is Ireland, you already
want more of it.
A high, wide, handsome house which is achingly comfortable and
astonishingly inexpensive, this is a place in which to do nothing very
much whatsoever — flop in front of the fire with a mind-emptying
mag, nap away the afternoon, focus on dinner for an hour beforehand
— or you could shoot and fish and do other estimable sporty fixations
should that be to your taste. Margaret Johnson makes it rather difficult
to drag yourself away from the house however, for she is a terrifically
sociable woman who makes you feel welcome in about thirty seconds
flat, whether you are jet-jaundiced or road-weary, or bright-eyed and
holiday-moded. Whatever your motivations Ballyteigue, with its
relaxed quirkiness and unpretentious ease, is somewhere splendid.

Open all year except Xmas
5 rooms, 4 en suite, single with private bathroom
Average Price: £17 per person
No Extra Charge
Credit Cards: Visa, Access/Master
Dinner, booked by noon £14
No Licence (bring your own wine)
No Wheelchair Access
Children — 50% reduction if sharing
Vegetarian meals available (notice required)
Pets by arrangement only (not in bedrooms)
Enclosed car park
1 hour from Shannon airport. Going towards Charleville on the Cork road, look out for
the Jet Petrol Station. Signposted from the next turn right.

B&B
DERRYAUN
Drummin, Westport, Co Mayo Tel: (098) 26885
Rebecca and Martin Rogan

Derryaun is a lovely little cottage — very little indeed: three bedrooms,
two of which interconnect so they are very useful for a young family,
and a sitting and dining room downstairs — but it has been tenderly
restored to create a sense of peace and relaxation, a sense of escapism,
which entirely suits this wild, organic environment. Derryaun is not so
far from the bright lights of Westport, but you could find yourself here,
walking and hiking and slowly driving around and about the environs
of the cottage, and think you were a million miles from anywhere that
boasted trippery tourists or the gee-gaws of the modern age.
Rebecca and Martin are vegetarians, and the breakfast here is
imaginative, indeed inspiring. A sample menu includes freshly
squeezed orange juice; a choice of cereals, muesli or granola; fresh
fruit with natural yogurt; mushroom and pine nut crêpes in a creamy
nutmeg sauce; French toast with fresh fruit and maple syrup; eggs
florentine, all offered with freshly baked muffins, scones or oven warm
soda bread. The coffee is freshly ground and there are ordinary or herbal
teas. The breakfast menu changes daily and organic vegetables are used
wherever possible. Everything is done thoughtfully and genuinely:
Derryaun is not some slick little episode which is part of the people
business: it is a thoughtful, consoling cottage, a place apart.

Open Apr-Sept
3 rooms (2 of which are adjoining, suitable for families), sharing 1 bathroom
Average Price: from £14 per person sharing, £17 single
No Extra Charges
No Credit Cards
No Restaurant (can recommend plenty locally)
No Licence
No Wheelchair Access
Children — welcome, 50% discount under 11yrs, free under 2yrs
Pets accommodated
Enclosed car park
Signposted from the N59 to Westport.

Country House
ENNISCOE HOUSE
Castlehill, Ballina, Co Mayo Tel: (096) 31112 Fax: 31773
Susan Kellett

Enniscoe is a relatively simple place, a modest country house which Susan Kellett is restoring slowly and lovingly, in a part of the country which is modest and under-celebrated. Things are done just right here, just so, and this desire to achieve correctness in simple things makes it a pleasurable house in which to while away some holiday time or an away-from-it-all weekend.

The bedrooms have enjoyed the same careful renovation which is re-energising the landings and common rooms of the house. Those at the front of the house, overlooking the grounds, are truly the ones you want to stay in, with their quirky four posters and big lazy canopy beds.

At dinnertime, local ingredients are dotted through the menu: a warm salad of black pudding and smoked bacon; roast pork with apricot and walnut sauce; brill with a carrot and chive sauce; roast lamb with a red wine sauce or maybe salmon with a white wine sauce, then a meringue cake or some old fashioned trifle. It is country house cooking, of course, but whilst in other places it might seem a little obvious, here the food feels just right, friendly food within a friendly house.

Best of all, Enniscoe is a place it is easy to relax in, a place to enjoy time alone and apart from the real world, a house that is polite, vivid and perfectly expressive of the strengths of Irish country house hospitality.

Open 1 Apr-14 Oct
6 rooms, 5 en suite, 1 with private bath
Average Price: £38-£50 per person sharing, £48-£54 single
No Extra Charges
Credit Cards: Visa, Access/Master, Amex
Open for dinner, book by noon, £20 (non resident booking by 10am, £20 plus 10% service charge)
Wine Licence
No Wheelchair Access
Children — high chair, cot, babysitting
Vegetarian meals available
Pets by arrangement only
Enclosed Car Park
Two miles south of Crossmolina on the road to Castlebar.

Country House
NEWPORT HOUSE
Newport, Co Mayo Tel: (098) 41222 Fax: 41613
Kieran & Thelma Thompson

Ceilings vault. Staircases cascade. Silences ascend. In the rooms the
women come and go, talking of Michelangelo. Where else could one be
but Newport House, that well-tuned anachronism in the modern world.
Newport is a fascinating kaleidoscope of clichés: the ruddy-cheeked
ghillies who wait around for fishing to begin, the impossibly stooped
gardener, the efficient Miss who counsels a full bowl of soup to
counteract intemperate August weather, the carrot headed waiter with
the full-time flushed cheeks, the ageing ladies who wait on the fringes
of the dining room and who, should you stay long enough, will elide
you under their wings and into their care.
Dinner is a lengthy affair that is firmly fin de siècle, except the century
is the 19th and not the 20th. Creamy soups will follow the wonderful
gravadlax. Turbot will enjoy a rich Champagne sauce, fresh salmon
might be char-grilled and the voluble flavours cut by fresh vegetables
from the walled garden behind the house. After some salad leaves, a
fine cheeseboard, and then a showypiece of desserts: crème caramel
under an Ascot hat of spun sugar, home-made ice-cream in a flighty
tuille basket.
Service is good, though some may find the dining room rather self-
consciously formal and quiet, full of well heeled Europeans: record
producers from Frankfurt, commercial lawyers, Frenchmen who went
to the right école, second rate politicians, each and all of them complete
with Trophy, or at least Reserve Prize, wives. In Newport's grand, billowy
rooms and in Newport's grand billowy bedrooms (the rooms in the house
are more covetable than those in the courtyard), they come and go, a
decorous distance always maintained. This is a formal house, and it
puts everyone on their best behaviour.

Open 19 Mar-6 Oct
19 rooms, all en suite
Average Price: £46-£60 per person sharing (single supplement £10)
No Extra Charges
Credit Cards: Visa, Access/Master, Amex, Diners
Restaurant open for dinner £28 (early evening dinner for kids)
Full Licence
Wheelchair Access (happy to help)
Children — high seats, cots, babysitting service
Vegetarian menu always available
Pets by arrangement
Enclosed car park
Newport House gates are to be found just at the entrance to the village.

Country House
PARTRY HOUSE
Ballinrobe, Co Mayo Tel: (092) 43004 Fax: 43138
Sally & David Shaw-Smith

Partry is a whacky, slightly scatty sort of house, enjoyably eccentric
in the manner of a Frank Capra movie or a Wodehouse country house
farce. In this solid and serious part of County Mayo, with its sternness
and Protestant plainness, the rush of giddy energy which is Partry is
wonderfully welcome.

The house itself, slowly being knocked into shape, is in a glorious
location set in 250 acres on the shores of Lough Carra: excellent for
brown trout fishing with salmon and sea trout fishing nearby, perfect
for exploring the unknowable reaches of Mayo. Inside, it is attractive
and femininely charming, not least for the giggly, girlish fecundities
of the fine Pauline Bewick paintings, and the warm colours of the
dining room.

Sally Shaw-Smith's breakfasts — fresh orange juice, a dollop of
porridge, then superbly scrambled eggs fresh as the Mayo air, sweet
field mushrooms, good fatty bacon, softly grilled tomato, crumbly and
dark soda bread and aromatic coffee — are deliciously flavourful and
restorative, for this is country in which to engage in energetic pursuits,
such as huntin', shootin' or fishin', or maybe on not doing very much
of anything at all.

Open all year except Xmas
5 rooms, none en suite
Average Price: £25 per person
No Service Charge. Boat available, £20; £40 with Ghillie and engine.
No Credit Cards
Dinner by arrangement £15, packed lunch £5
Wine Licence
No Wheelchair access
Children — by arrangement only
Wide variety of Vegetarian food available
Pets accommodated
Private Car park
3 miles from Ballinrobe. Take the Castlebar road and, having passed the Keel river bridge,
look for the estate entrance on the right. Arched entrance and gate-lodge on bend.

Guesthouse
ROSTURK WOODS
Rosturk, Mulrany, Co Mayo Tel & Fax: (098) 36264
Louisa and Alan Stoney

Out in the wild and wet west, just before you cross over onto the
surreal embrace of Achill, Louisa and Alan Stoney's house is highly
regarded for its peaceable and private nature and the understated
comfort of well chosen furnishings, carefully considered things.
Mrs Stoney cooks breakfasts and dinners with equal fastidiousness,
and her energy and enthusiasm makes Rosturk a valuable place.

Open Apr-end Oct (out of season by arrangement)
6 double rooms
Average Price: £12-£25 per person
No Service Charge.
Credit Cards: Visa, Access/Master
Dinner for guests, £21
Wine Licence
No Wheelchair access
Children — welcome
Vegetarian options available on request
No pets in house
Private Car park
Seven miles west of Newport.

Country House
HILTON PARK ★
Scotshouse, Co Monaghan Tel: (047) 56007 Fax: 56033
Johnny and Lucy Madden

Hilton Park is chalumeau calm, a seductive place, a palette for Johnny
and Lucy Madden to assemble the gallimaufry of country house
gestures, pitching them together to create a canvas of aching pleasure.
The house offers vast Princess-and-the-Pea beds, yawning big baths,
halls, landings and rooms painted in roaring red and deep greens that
come alive with splendour when the evening sun rushes through the
windows. A dining room of classical elegance is counterpointed by a
downstairs breakfast room of ruddy efficacy. In total, this array of
features makes for a house which is a paragon of desirability. 'For me,
that place is perfection', a recent visitor — unasked — volunteered.
Johnny and Lucy Madden supply the artistry and the ingenuity which
make Hilton what it is, but their work would be nothing without the
devoted persistence that underlies their efforts. Lucy Madden's food
reveals a cook with an instinctive feel for ingredients, many of them
coming from her own organic garden and she has the skill to make
food expressive and volatile: no moribund beef and spuds here, instead
that fillet of beef will match with a perfect bearnaise that will match
the sharp clean sweetness of garden asparagus, following an antipasti
of roasted peppers and before some salad and farmhouse cheese and
fresh fruit. She is a hungry cook, hungry to experiment, hungry to
invent, with an autodidact's devotion to learning that is being gradually
put to use in the book of potato recipes she is writing.
Johnny Madden himself has just the right sort of nonchalance, not to
mention celebrated skills in the kitchen himself at breakfast time, to
match this big pile, preventing it from seeming even remotely
fossilised, gifting it with a young sense of humour.

Open Apr-Sept
5 rooms, all en suite
Average Price: £55.50 per person, £5 single supplement
No Extra Charges
Credit Cards: Visa, Access/Master
Dinner for residents only, book by noon, £22.50
Wine Licence
No Wheelchair Access
Children — by arrangement only
Vegetarian meals available (24 hour's notice please)
No pets in house
Enclosed car park
Three miles out of Clones on the L46 to Ballyhaise, the entrance gates are dark
green with silver falcons.

Country House
TULLANISK
Birr, Co Offaly Tel: (0509) 20572
Susie & George Gossip

You would have to like anywhere run by a couple with the thrillingly promising name of Gossip, and George and Susie's country house, on the Birr Castle estate, has acquired many admirers of its comfortable and handsome rooms, the crack of the communal dinners, the calming fact that here, in the middle of the country, you feel happily in the middle of nowhere.

Indeed, this admiration can provoke the purplest of prose, the most breathless recounts of weekends, and romantically alluring accounts of pleasureful times. Perhaps it has been the true-tasting and quietly ingenious procession of food enjoyed at dinner, with good wines and good chat to aid the flow of the evening, or kidneys and pudding and fruit ready to be scooped off the sideboard at breakfast. Maybe it's the elegant bedrooms with their crisp cotton sheets or the flowers and posies that are everywhere. Whatever it is, no sooner has someone come back from Tullanisk than they are dying to advocate it, with infectious enthusiasm, to everyone they know.

There is plenty of golfing, shooting, riding, trekking and walking to be done but George and Susie reckon, wisely, that 'you can please yourself and do just as much, or just as little, as you like'. In these over-heated times, that may be one of the best offers you are likely to get.

Open all year except Xmas and the month of Feb
7 rooms, 5 en suite
Average Price: £32-£42 per person sharing, single supplement £7
No Extra Charges
Credit Cards: Visa, Access
Dinner available, £20, book by noon
Wine Licence
Wheelchair Access (1 room downstairs, help offered with step)
Children — welcome
Vegetarian meals provided (please give notice when booking)
Pets allowed (but not in bedrooms)
Enclosed car park
Signposted from the Banaher Road.

Country House
COOPERSHILL HOUSE
Riverstown, Co Sligo Tel: (071) 65108 Fax: 65466
Brian and Lindy O'Hara

Coopershill can seem a slightly serious sort of house, somewhere likely
to have people putting on their best behaviour, their public faces, even
with Brian O'Hara's droll and dry sense of humour working hard to put
everyone at their ease. Perhaps it is because dinner is taken at separate
tables, rather than in communion with your fellow guests, which breaks
up the spell of pre-dinner drinks, or maybe it is simply the type of people
who are attracted to Coopershill, folk for whom social diplomacies are
very important.

Yet, despite this, it is hard to escape the surreal qualities of Coopershill,
and impossible not to find amusement and humour in them. These
serious other guests, for example, always impress as people with
interesting other lives — is this why they put on their public faces? —
people with pasts, curious presents. Teasing a little of their mystery
out of them over the course of a belter of a brandy after dinner is a joy,
though some ill-informed and inaccurate speculation about them as
you enjoy Lindy's cooking during dinner will do nicely.

They give a country weekend party feel to Coopershill, an Agatha
Christie edge, and everything else about the house, the peacocks, the
peacefulness — when the peacocks aren't bleating — the out-of-time
atmosphere, colludes with this. Coopershill allows you to enter a
mystery movie by Merchant and Ivory, a Henry James whodunnit.

Open mid Mar-end Oct (out of season house parties by arrangement, incl. Xmas and
New Year)
6 rooms, all en suite
Average Price: £42 per person sharing, £50 single
No Extra Charges
Credit Cards: Access/Master, Visa, Amex
Dinner for guests only, book by noon, £21
Wine Licence
No Wheelchair Access
Children — high seats, cots, babysitting service
Vegetarian meals available (give notice please)
No pets in the house   Enclosed car park
Coopershill is clearly signposted from the Drumfin crossroads on the N4, 11 miles
southwest of Sligo.

Country House
CROMLEACH LODGE
Ballindoon, Boyle, Co Sligo Tel: (071) 65155 Fax: 65455
Christy and Moira Tighe

Neither Christy nor Moira Tighe have a background in the business of
running a restaurant with rooms but their determination to improve,
their will to succeed, has meant that Cromleach has steadily acquired
an impressive reputation over the last few years, become a monument
to painstaking application.

From a distance the house itself is a curious concoction, reflecting the
fact that it is the sum of steady accretions over the years, with the
original building now difficult to detect amidst the extra rooms and
dining rooms which have been added.

The bedrooms upstairs are super-large and super-comfortable with
heartbreak views across fields that appear to have been purloined from
a painting by Breughel, and on and out across Lough Arrow and the
gorgeous Curlew Mountains.

Moira Tighe's cooking exploits two central themes: impeccable
ingredients from local growers, the bulk of the vegetables and herbs
being organically grown, and cooking which, despite the fact that she
is self taught, strides confidently between modern improvisations and
the classic verities where her work can seem most confidently at home.
Whatever she does, this is a cook with personality and Cromleach is a
house where one is always aware of the hard-working presence of
Christy and Moira Tighe, and their determination to do things right.

Open all year Xmas and 2 weeks in Jan
10 rooms, all en suite
Average Price: from £40-£62 per person, £15 single supplement
No Extra Charges
Credit Cards: Visa, Access, Amex
Restaurant open for dinner, £26.50
Full Licence
Wheelchair Access only with assistance
Children — welcome
Vegetarian food always available
No pets
Enclosed car park
Cromleach Lodge is signposted on the A4 just after you leave Boyle, heading west.

Restaurant with Accommodation
GLEBE HOUSE
Coolaney Road, Collooney, Co Sligo Tel: (071) 67787
Brid and Marc Torrades

Brid and Marc Torrades read a newspaper article about Glebe House, at
the time a splendid ruin in Collooney, near Sligo, and with the wild energy
of youth they immediately migrated to the west coast and to the prospect
of two years solid slog to bring the unruly ruin back to some kind of shape.
By August 1990, they were open for business, quickly achieving
popularity amongst the well-fed citizens of Sligo, a fame which has
since spread steadily, by stealthy word of mouth. That quiet fame is
well founded, for Ms Torrades allies a tenderly feminine skill as a cook
with a rock-solid appreciation of fresh ingredients, most of them grown
in the garden at Glebe by Marc.
She cooks with great motivation, with the rustic element of cuisine
bourgeois perhaps most at home in her culinary scheme: leg of lamb
with Madeira, or sautéed beef with wild mushrooms and garlic are
lovable confections of hers, the kind of dishes you want to eat on
autumn evenings, when you will pray that the parsnips are in season,
for I once ate a purée of parsnips here that made the hairs on the back
of my neck stand to attention it was so divine, so right.
These combinations, and many of her other favoured dishes, are timeless
but the sparkling quality of the ingredients which Marc Torrades grows
and Brid's contented and understated style make them seem brand new.
The rooms in the house are simple, and inexpensive, for Mr and Mrs
Torrades are still walking their financial tightrope, and improvements to
the house happen steadily rather than in any shocking burst. No matter.
It is the food and the hospitality and the energetic cheerfulness which is
the charm of Glebe, and that charm is considerable.

Open all year except 2 weeks Jan
5 rooms, all en suite
Average Price: £16 per person sharing, £20 single
No Extra Charges
Credit Cards: Visa, Access/Master, Amex
Restaurant open from 6pm, £16 (light meals available)
Wine Licence
No Wheelchair Access
Children — high chair, cot, babysitting, children's playroom and outside play area
(please advise of needs when booking)
Vegetarian meals always available
Pets accommodated, but not in bedrooms
Enclosed Car Park
Glebe House is signposted from the main Dublin/Sligo road.

Country Castle
MARKREE CASTLE
Collooney, Co Sligo Tel: (071) 67800 Fax: 67840
Charles and Mary Cooper

Markree may appear to be an imposing sort of place as you see it for
the first time, winding your way to it along the snaking drive, somewhere
Gothic dark and eerily forbidding. In fact, it is actually a shy, nervous
sort of castle: in cinematic terms we would have to say it is more Rocky
Horror than Hammer Horror, Disneyland innocent rather than a
boastful Citizen Kane-style Xanadu.

Charles and Mary Cooper's painstaking restoration is beginning to raise
Markree from its decades of neglect, when it all but tumbled to the
ground, and whilst there remain echoes of boarding school colours here
and there, and some of the rooms could enjoy a little more decorative
spice, Markree is agreeable and, ironically, extravagantly simple.

The food in the Knockmuldowney Restaurant is country house modest
— mussels in herb butter, baked rabbit, lemon soufflé — but flavours
are good, and the wine list is expansive and inexpensive and a real treat
for the serious quaffer. Breakfast, in the brightness of the dining room
with the babble of foreign tongues all around you and the comfort of
solicitous Sligo ladies ushering food to the table, is charming.

Open all year except Xmas and Feb
14 rooms, all en suite
Average Price: £43.50-£48.50 per person sharing, £53.50-£58.50 single
No Extra Charges
Credit Cards: Visa, Access/Master, Amex, Diners
Restaurant open for dinner, £19.50 and £22.50
Restaurant Licence
No Wheelchair Access
Children — welcome but no special menus, babysitting
Vegetarian meals on request and by discussion
Pets welcome
Private Car Park
Markree Castle is clearly signposted from the N4.

Self-Catering Cottages

NETTLE COTTAGES

Ballincastle, Cliffoney, Co Sligo Tel: (071) 66399
Hans and Gaby Wieland

Hans and Gaby grind flour, bake breads and cheesecakes, make cheese from cow's and goat's milk, grow vegetables organically and rent out their cottages, and they do everything with disarming charm and, best of all, with the joyous peal of Gaby's laughter adding a note of frothy irresistibility to their work. The bread, the cheesecake, the cheeses are all filled with joie de vivre, filled with the lovely flavour of zestful love of life.

There is an easy way to enjoy the plenitude of their hard work, but to do so you must act quickly. Hans and Gaby's little cottages book up quickly, quickly. Not just because their location is perfect, of course, though that counts. It is also because the cottages are sweetness themselves: cosy and inviting, just right for holiday energy and weekends-away. You might decide, faced with this bounty and this comfort, to explore no more than yourself when in Nettle Cottages.

Open all year
2 self-catering cottages: Cottage 1 with one bedroom under open loft for extra sleeping space, Cottage 2 with one bedroom with open loft in the living room, fitted kitchen and bathroom
Average Price: per week Jan-Mar (1) £80, (2) £100; Apr-May (1) £100, (2) £120; Jun-Sept (1) £120, (2) £140; Oct-Dec (1) £100, (2) £120
Extra Charges: Electricity and logs for heating
No Credit Cards
Cheese, bread, milk, quark, cheesecake and organic vegetables for sale
Children — welcome
Recommended for Vegetarians
No pets
Enclosed car park
Up the narrow road on the right before the Sligo end of Cliffoney.

Country House

TEMPLE HOUSE ★ £
Ballymote, Co Sligo Tel: (071) 83329 Fax: 83808
Sandy and Deb Perceval

The word you most often hear in connection with Temple House is
'perfection'. Nothing more, nothing less. The ability of Sandy and Deb
Perceval and this hulkingly handsome house to render people almost
speechless with delight is unchallenged in Ireland.

What do people love? The food, says the acclaimed chef. The dinner
party atmosphere, say your parents. The whacky and exotic rooms,
say your friends, and they list the contents of the Twins' Room: two
emerald porcelain washbasins, two wash stands, two bed-end tables,
two bedside lamps, two bedside polar bear ornaments, two towels,
two flannels, two windows and two fine canopied beds. The friendship,
say the people who have already been three times. The sport, say the
fishermen and the huntsmen. Temple House is all things to all men
and women, and all these things spell happiness.

The house itself is an artful confection, undeniably absurd and
splendid, but it is the Perceval's gift to remove any strain of
preciousness or pretention from Temple House which makes it work,
and makes it appeal to those who love country houses and those who
loathe them. Deb Perceval's cooking is an important element of the
magic, for she manages always to produce dinners which are exactly
appropriate, both for the evening and for the people with whom you
share dinner: an onion and blue cheese tart, some of the farm pork in
a fillet with a basil sauce, a chocolate meringue gâteau. 'They are able
to create a real kind of relaxed caring', says the lady from Germany
sitting across from you at dinner. Yes, that's it. Do note that one is
politely requested to refrain from wearing perfumes and after shaves,
as they engender an allergic reaction in Mr Perceval.

Open 1 Apr-30 Nov
5 rooms, 4 en suite, 1 private bathroom
Average Price: £35 per person sharing, £40 single
Optional Service Charge
Credit Cards: Visa, Access/Master, Amex
Dinner for guests only £17, book by noon
Wine Licence
No Wheelchair Access
Children — high chairs, cots, babysitting
Recommended for Vegetarians with prior notice
Pets welcome, but not in house
Private Car Park
Temple House is 14 miles from Sligo and is signposted from the N17. Travellers from
Dublin follow signs from ESSO garage in Ballymote.

B&B

HANORA'S COTTAGE

Nire Valley, Clonmel, Co Waterford Tel: (052) 36134 Fax: 25145
Eoin Wall

Waterford, a small county, a quiet, enclosed sort of place is aptly named — Water Ford. The feel of flowing water is paramount, from the strong rush of Waterford Harbour which dominates its eastern side and gives a seastruck air to the cute towns of Dunmore East and Passage East, to the rivers which thread through the valleys at the northern end of the county, criss-crossed by stone bridges.

Snuggled within the silent embrace of one of the Comeragh mountain valleys, Hanora's Cottage overlooks the river Nire and is overlooked itself by the Nire church, set slightly higher at the foot of the mountains.

Eoin Wall — a Ballymaloe School trained chef — carefully sources good foods for the breakfasts and dinners that add the final touch of quietude to this quiet place. Breakfast bacon comes from the Rudds in County Offaly, while local organic grower Vicky Heslop supplies him with vegetables.

Open all year except Xmas
8 rooms, 4 en suite
Average Price: £18.50 per person sharing
Credit Cards: Visa, Access/Master, Amex, Diners
Dinner by arrangement, £15
Wine Licence
No Wheelchair Access
Children — welcome
Vegetarian breakfast available
No pets
Car park
Turn off the Clonmel/Dungarvan road at Ballymacarby.

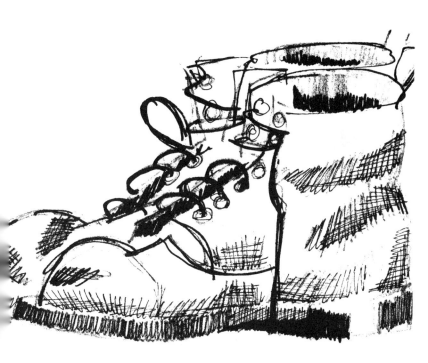

B&B

FURZIESTOWN HOUSE

Tacumshane, Co Wexford Tel: (053) 31376
Yvonne Pim

It is the instinctive thoughtfulness she brings to everything that makes Yvonne Pim's house so special. Furziestown is little more than a nice farmhouse way down here in the heel of the country, but Mrs Pim's care and concern for her guests has elevated the house into one of the most highly regarded places to stay in the country. You feel welcome. Mrs Pim spoils you. You love it.

And you will love the food: one dinner began with Scandinavian fish mousse, then organic roast lamb with garden herbs, served with steamed scarlet runner beans, broad beans in a light bechamel sauce and roast potatoes, with rosemary and crab apple jelly and fresh mint sauce to garnish, before a bombe of summer berries. Mrs Pim also does menus for vegetarians — mushroom croustades on a bed of mixed greens, chick peas in spiced lentil and coconut sauce with mixed rice, then a carrageen moss mousse — and for vegans — carrot and apple salad, then sesame tofu with stir-fried vegetables and mixed rice with courgettes and cashews. Many travellers who stay their first night with Mrs Pim find that they must, just must, spend their last night at Furziestown also. True, the location is ideal, but that isn't why people return. Furziestown provides a microcosm of all that is good about Ireland and, with the parting embrace of good food and instinctive hospitality to glide you on your way, leaving doesn't seem quite so bad after all. One friend described Furziestown to us as 'perfect', and that may just be right.

Open Mar-Nov
3 rooms, all en suite
Average Price: £15 per person, no single supplement
No Extra Charges
No Credit Cards
Dinner available, £12.50 3-course, £10 2-course, book previous day
No Licence (bring your own)
No Wheelchair Access, but 2 downstairs bedrooms suitable for disabled
Children — high chairs, cots, and babysitting whenever possible
Recommended for Vegetarians
Pets welcome, but not in bedrooms
Enclosed Car Park
Signposted from Tacumshane.

Farmhouse Accommodation

HORETOWN HOUSE

Foulksmills, Co Wexford Tel: (051) 63706 Fax: 63633
Ivor Young

Horetown is a plain old pile of a country house, catholic in its capaciousness, Calvinistic in its plainness, and it comes as little surprise to discover that its history interlinks with Cromwell — who granted the townland of Horetown to William Goffe, a puritan — and later on with the Quakers.

The house, then, exudes the power of wealth, but in no way betrays a passion for money, so one's final impression is of somewhere defiantly Victorian, proud of power but ambiguous about riches.

This curious architectural ambience is met, inside, by a sort of Arsenic and Old Lace plainness: Horetown feels like the sort of house a maiden aunt might own, and has just the sort of time-dated accoutrements of unsophisticated plumbing and heating which your aunt might have installed in the 1950s. It is eccentric, quite gloriously so, and whilst some love this, some do not.

Downstairs, the Cellar Restaurant has a kick-off-your-shoes, devil-may-care character, which explains why so many people enjoy coming here time and again, and Ivor Young's straightforward, easy-going food is old-fashioned and welcoming.

Open all year except Xmas and the month of Feb
12 rooms, none en suite
Average Price: £22 per person sharing
No Extra Charges
No Credit Cards
Restaurant open for dinner
Wine Licence
No Wheelchair Access
Children — welcome
Vegetarian meals available (notice always helps)
No pets
Enclosed car park
From Wexford, turn left in Taghmon village (opp. Furlong's), drive for exactly 3.5 miles on the L160 to Horetown House sign.

Country House
NEWBAY HOUSE
Newbay, Co Wexford Tel: (053) 42779 Fax: 24318
Paul & Mientje Drumm

What kind of place is Newbay? It is the kind of place where, after a
splendid breakfast, you might decide that the best thing to do to get
the day rolling would be to, well, just go right back to bed. And so you
do, with a clear conscience and, with the lightsome light of Wexford
filtering through the curtains when you wake up a couple of hours
later, you might decide that this was one of your most inspired
decisions.

That's the kind of place Newbay is, one of the most relaxing and
convivial of the country houses. Partly this comes from Min Drumm's
social skills and the expert ease with which she sets everyone into the
pace of the house as they sip sherries as a prelude to dinner. Partly, its
the unpretentious design of the house, the light sense of space thanks
to the stripped pine furniture — a speciality of Paul Drumm's.

But it is also the excellent cooking: well judged, both interesting and
satisfying, a cross between professional assurance and an amateurish
charm. On a good night, with the big table ringed by happy diners
gaustering away one to the other and the food and wine flowing
seamlessly, it is perfectly charming.

Open all year except Xmas
6 rooms, all en suite
Average Price: £29 per person sharing, £37 single
No Extra Charges
Credit Cards: Visa, Access/Master
Dinner for guests, £25, book by noon
Wine Licence (and bring your own)
No Wheelchair Access
Children — no facilities
Not suitable for Vegetarians
No pets in house
Enclosed Car Park
Newbay House is signposted from the N25 which curls around Wexford town.

Townhouse
McMENAMIN'S TOWNHOUSE
3 Auburn Terrace, Redmond Road, Wexford, Co Wexford Tel: (053) 46442
Seamus & Kay McMenamin

The McMenamins run a friendly and efficacious house, close to the
centre of town. The staggering choice of foods available at breakfast —
including some super-duper fish — is almost overwhelming in its
largesse: a bumper of breads, fruits, juices, eggs anywhichway,
steaming coffee and wake-up tea.
Seamus and Kay are professional people persons, with the confidence of
many years in the pub business gifting them with the ability to know
just what it is you would like, even before you have fully decided what
it is you would like yourself. The collection of beds which grace the
various rooms, some of them of very great value, add an extra sheen
to the house which works perfectly as a base for first night-last night
stays, thanks to its proximity to Rosslare, but also for the Opera
Festival and for enjoyably aimless meandering through the Sunny
South-East.

Open all year (except Xmas)
6 rooms, all en suite
Average Price: £16.50 per person
No Extra Charges
Credit Cards: Visa, Access/Master
Will book restaurants locally
No Licence
No Wheelchair Access
Children — welcome, cot provided
Vegetarian food on request
No pets
Private Parking
Opposite the railway station.

Country House
SALVILLE HOUSE ➡
Enniscorthy, Co Wexford Tel: (054) 35252
Jane and Gordon Parker

We arrived at Salville one evening to discover, even before we had walked into the house, that the face at the upstairs window was that of a friend. Twenty minutes later, two other friends arrived who were also staying the night in this quietly inspiring house. While this sort of freak occurrence helps to give somewhere a country-house-weekend feel, with you and your mates happily colliding together to have a good time, Salville is actually the kind of house that will engender these sort of time-off feelings, whether or not you have known your fellow guests for five minutes or five years.

It is a simply lovely house, sat snug on a hill overlooking a wood, scarcely decorated in the nouveau pauvre style, with excellent food from dinner to breakfast to the revivifying cup of tea when you get together with your friends and say 'Fancy meeting you here!'. Meeting your friends does have the added benefit of the fact that you can show each other your splendid bedrooms, with their massive windows ushering in masses of bright light.

Its location is perfect: close enough to the ferry at Rosslare to allow you to glide up to Enniscorthy and settle into that youthsome holiday spirit in double-quick time. Close enough to Wexford to allow easy access to the Opera festival, a mere scoot down from Dublin to allow you to unwind from workday worries and settle into the hush and easy hustle of the country.

Open all year except Xmas Day
3 rooms sharing 1 bathroom plus self-catering guest wing (2 bedrooms)
Average Price: £15 per person. Self-catering wing from £110 per week
No extra charges
No Credit Cards
Dinner, £15 if pre-booked
No Licence (bring your own)
Wheelchair Access (telephone to discuss details)
Children — welcome
Vegetarian food always available (happy to discuss menus when booking)
Pets only with guests staying in self-contained wing
Car park
Just off the N11 to Wexford — take the first left after the hospital, go up the hill to a T-junction then turn left and proceed for one third of a mile.

Country House
THE OLD RECTORY
Wicklow, Co Wicklow Tel: (0404) 67048 Fax: 69181
Paul and Linda Saunders

In Linda Saunders, one meets a person who is something of an aleph of
County Wicklow. A vital and essential asset to the town and the county,
her character seems to sum up this delightful place — quietly complex,
slightly reserved, but pretty bloody determined behind it all — and her
effusive and intricate cooking is a perfect reflection of the strengths
and delights of Wicklow.
She uses fine organic ingredients, grown locally, and this explains firstly
why her food always has a vibrancy and freshness about it.
To this, she brings a degree of invention and expressiveness — and an
intellectual comprehension and understanding of the architecture of taste
— which few other country house cooks can match. Indeed, this sense
of complex but compatible flavouring in her food is reminiscent of the
structure of a perfume, with alluring scents and mellifluous taste structures
to be enjoyed both in main dishes and in their compatriot sauces: a warm
terrine of salmon and sea trout will swim along with a green herb sauce,
parsnips will pair off with red beans for a soup, whilst the elegant ruddiness
of a carrot and cucumber tart will have the warm spice of marjoram.
But there is more to Linda Saunders' skill than just the ability to
conjure intricate tastes with skill. She also, bravely, can construct
entire dinner menus to arrive at compatibility and complexity and,
to celebrate the Wicklow Flower Festival, cooks a dauntingly daring
ten course Floral Dinner.
The extension of the dining room has gifted the Old Rectory with greater
light, perfect for a cuisine of such delicacy, and Paul Saunders' intelligent
collection of wines is terrifically promising, with an unusual account of
good Spanish wines. Rooms in the house are cosy comfy, and whilst the
Rectory is a good base for exploring Wicklow, you will likely find that
you will want to eat nowhere else but here.

Open 1 Apr-31 Oct
5 rooms, all en suite
Average Price: £44 per person sharing, £64 single
No Extra Charges
Credit Cards: Visa, Access/Master, Amex, Diners
Restaurant open Sun-Thur 8pm, Fri-Sat 7.30pm-9pm, booking essential
Wine Licence
No Wheelchair Access
Children — welcome
Recommended for Vegetarians
No pets
Enclosed Car Park
30 miles south of Dublin (45 mins), on the left hand side of the road as you enter
Wicklow town, heading South.

Country House
RATHSALLAGH HOUSE
Dunlavin, Co Wicklow Tel: (045) 53112 Fax: 53343
Joe and Kay O'Flynn

'Dear Mr & Mrs McKenna, My husband and I spent five glorious days last week at the Rathsallagh House and we look forward to returning every year, if possible'.

So began a letter from the 'States which, after this enthusiastic encomium, went on to roundly denounce us for failing to express ourselves in the language of devotional delight which the adherents of Rathsallagh use to describe their favourite place. And my goodness but they are effusive and devoted to this lovely house, and to the fine dinners and breakfasts which Joe and Kay O'Flynn prepare. Mention to them that you feel prices in Rathsallagh are steep and they will look at you with incredulity, as if to say: What price perfection?

The secret of Rathsallagh is, surely, that it feels like an enclave, a cosy enclave of civilisation, set apart from the barbarous world. It is this feeling that so captivates people, the impression that everything elsewhere has ceased to exist, and this bubble of wooded grounds, misty mornings, fireside breakfasts, the coven of the courtyard rooms and the roisterous dinners is a magical mysteryland, all on its own. A masterly illusion, when you consider that Dublin City is scarcely up the road, but a narcotic one.

Open all year, except Xmas
14 rooms, all en suite
Average Price: £55-£85 per person sharing
No Extra Charges
Credit Cards: Amex, Visa, Access/Master
Restaurant open 7.30pm-8.30pm
Full pub Licence
No Wheelchair Access
Children— over 12 years welcome
Vegetarian meals available (please give notice)
No pets
Enclosed car park
Signposted from Dunlavin Village.

Country House
TINAKILLY HOUSE HOTEL
Rathnew, Co Wicklow Tel: (0404) 69274 Fax: 67806
William & Bee Power

They are great sports, William and Bee Power. You might think that
the slog — the hard slog — of running a well-run country house
throughout the year might allow them, come Christmas time, to pile
their feet up and pour themselves, rather than someone else, a drink.
Not a bit of it. Christmas at Tinakilly is bright with the same sort of
merriment the Powers bring to their year-round task and, perhaps
appropriately in this big old Victorian pile of a house, the theme they
adopt is Dickensian: pots of punch, a plenitude of goose and turkey
and plum pud, ponies and traps and smoochy mistletoe and, doubtless,
someone offering Tiny Tim's salutation: 'God bless us everyone!'.
For the rest of the year, the Powers-that-be allow this thoughtfulness
to infiltrate the house wholesale: good menus and a kitchen which is
happy to prepare dishes plainly, a good wine list with plenty of half-
bottles and lots of clarets, plenty of peace and quiet and comfort if
you want it in both the house and the acres of gardens.
'Ambience and service are first class', a gentleman wrote to us once,
just one voice in a consistent chorus.

Open all year incl Xmas and New Year
29 rooms, all with full private facilities
Average Price: £50-£85 per person sharing, £75 single
No Extra Charges
Credit Cards: Visa, Access/Master, Amex, Diners
Dinner, £27.50, booking essential (open to non-residents)
Full Pub Licence
Wheelchair Access (incl disabled bathroom)
Children — high chairs, cots, babysitting by prior arrangement
Vegetarian meals with prior notice
No pets
Private Car Park
The House is signposted from Rathnew.

NORTHERN IRELAND
CONTENTS

Guesthouse
ASH ROWAN
12 Windsor Avenue, Belfast BT9 6EE Tel: (0232) 661758 Fax: 663227
Sam & Evelyn Hazlett

Ash Rowan is a relaxed, old-style house, welcoming and extra-friendly, a balm for the road-frazzled and the business-lagged, a place ever popular with visitors to Belfast who won't tolerate the city's bland hotels, visitors who seek the personal touch.

The efficiency and thoughtfulness of the house is as charming as the Hazletts themselves, the hearty breakfasts are fine and fulsome, with Irish scramble — eggs with chopped bacon and mushrooms — or smoked kippers or the Full Irish Fry ('Not for the faint hearted', warns the menu!) and the fact that you can even enjoy it late in the morning if pre-arranged. There are the morning papers to peruse and fret over, and a peaceful atmosphere to set you up for the day.

The location of the house is perfect, though Windsor Avenue is by no means as peaceful a place as it used to be, comprising nowadays a slew of schools, crêches and discreet Government offices. But whether you find yourself in the northern capital on business or pleasure, here you are situate near to everything worthwhile in the city.

You can literally stroll downtown to the restaurants and pubs, while being a matter of minutes from the Westlink means that access to and egress from Belfast is a cinch. This is a good place for either a first or last night if you are leaving from the ports of Belfast or Larne. It is also one of the nicest parts of town: leafy, a little sedate, a little out of time. Just like Ash Rowan

Open all year except 2 weeks at Xmas
5 rooms, all en suite
Average Price: £28-£33 per person sharing, £38-£46 single
No Extra charges
Credit Cards: Visa, Access/Master
No Restaurant
No Licence
No Wheelchair Access
Children — over 12yrs welcome
Vegetarian breakfast always available
No pets
Enclosed car park
Windsor Avenue runs between the Lisburn Road and the Malone Road.

Guesthouse
MALONE GUEST HOUSE
79 Malone Road, Belfast BT9 6SH Tel: (0232) 669565
Elsie McClure

Number 79 sits smack bang on the Malone Road, a matter of minutes from Queens University, the breezy vivacity of Botanic Avenue and Shaftesbury Square, close to all the best things of the city and in one of the nicest parts of town.

It is a solid, bourgeois, red brick house, as indeed are most of the houses all around and about it, houses that once were testament to the wealth of their owners. The character and complexion of the Malone Road has changed a lot over the last three decades, but it still hangs on to a well-fed, well-pleased-with-itself sort of air, an air of satisfaction which even the proximity of droves of revolting students — the halls of residence of Queens are just down the road — hasn't dented too much. Elsie McClure's B&B is one of the best regarded and best established, and probably the best-located, places to stay in town. It is a pleasing, affable house, replete, of course, with good Northern officiousness and maternal concern, and it represents fine value for money: there are few places of much character to stay in so near to the city, so number 79 is a vital antidote to the dread hotels of the city centre.

Open all year, except Xmas and mid-July
8 rooms, all en suite
Average Price: Mon-Thur £30 single, £45 twin, Fri-Sun £23 single, £37 twin
No Extra Charges
No Credit Cards
No Restaurant
No Licence
No Wheelchair Access
Children — no facilities
Vegetarian meals available (please give notice)
No pets
Enclosed car park
On the right hand side of the road as you drive away from the University, just past the BP Station.

Guesthouse
OAK HILL COUNTRY HOUSE
59 Dunmurry Lane, Belfast BT17 9JR Tel: (0232) 610658
May Noble

May Noble's expansive Victorian house is perhaps the grandest private house to stay in in the capital of the north, though it is actually a few miles out of the city centre, up in the well-heeled area of Dunmurry. This is an archetypal Victorian bourgeois family home, almost forbidding in its grand scale and with every feature unapologetically statuesque, and immaculately maintained by Mrs Noble. The views from the bedrooms across the gardens are achingly fine and contenting for the soul, and, once again, they are immaculately maintained.
The assiduous housekeeping, the calming grounds and the almost swollen sense of comfort one feels here can make it all to hard to leave, when it comes time to leave.

Open all year, except Xmas
4 rooms, all en suite
Average Price: per room £50 single, £70 double
No Extra Charges
No Credit Cards
Dinner by arrangement, book by 4pm, £15
No Licence
No Wheelchair Access
Children — cots and extra beds in family rooms
Vegetarian meals available (please give notice)
No pets
Enclosed car park
Adjacent to Belfast's Outer Ring — telephone for precise instructions.

Restaurant with Rooms

AUBERGE DE SENEIRL

28 Ballyclough Rd, Bushmills, Co Antrim Tel: (02657) 41536
Barbara Defres

The Auberge can seem a somewhat surreal experience in the context of the North, with its menus in gothic script and the curious, introverted atmosphere of the small dining room. In provincial France it would not seem anything like so strange, for the concept of opening a dining room for the public in a converted house, or, indeed, in a converted schoolhouse, as this is, is relatively commonplace in areas like the Dordogne.

But, near Bushmills, this strangeness is pleasing, and Barbara Defres' cooking, with its understated but closely understood idea of simple French food, is unexpected and enjoyable. Mrs Defres sticks to classic fare — smoked trout with horseradish, goat's cheese on croûtons, poached chicken with a tarragon sauce, Barbary duck, pastry creams and gâteaux for dessert — and with the small wine list and the quiet service it makes for a nice space. The five bedrooms in the house are a boon to the diner who is also a quaffer and who does not wish to run the gauntlet of the drink-driving laws and there is also a swimming pool for those who, having plunged in, may want to plunge in some more, not to mention a sauna and a solarium.

Open all year
5 rooms, all en suite (1 suite with jacuzzi)
Average Price: £43-£74 per room, sharing
No Extra Charges
Credit Cards: Amex, Diners
Restaurant open for dinner
Full Licence
No Wheelchair Access
Children — high chairs, baby listening machines
Vegetarian meals only with prior notice
No pets
Enclosed Car Park
The Auberge is signposted from the B67 and the B147

Farmhouse
MADDYBENNY FARM HOUSE
18 Maddybenny Park, Portrush, Co Antrim Tel: (0265) 823394
Rosemary White

Rosemary White's breakfast presents an agonising drama of multiple
choice. Before you head off to sleep you need to fill in the breakfast
menu to give them some idea of what you want to eat.
First of all, the porridge. You can have it your way or The Maddybenny
Way. The Maddybenny Way is to serve the grains with runny honey,
either Drambuie or Irish Mist, and lashings of cream. You'll have it
The Maddybenny Way.
Then, the agony of decision continues. Which main dish will it be?
The Ulster Fry, with soda and fadge? Kipper fillets poached in lemon
juice and dill? Trout braised in lemon butter, then served with smoked
bacon and mushrooms? Maybe a smoked haddock ramekin? Or lamb's
kidneys? Boiled eggs? Scrambled eggs?
You could flunk the responsibility, of course, and just content
yourself with the fresh soda bread and toast, the handmade jams and
marmalades, the country butter, a clatter of cups of Earl Grey, or maybe
some hot chocolate. But, once the choice is made, sleep will be bound
to be sound with plenty to look forward to when you wake.
In every other way, Mrs White will make life easy for you. They
helpfully arrange bookings in local restaurants, know all and sundry
about all and sundry which could possibly be of interest locally and,
if you are brave enough, you can hack out with a pony from their
riding centre.

Open all year except 2 weeks at Xmas
3 rooms, all en suite
Average Price: £18.50 per person sharing, £23 single
No Extra Charges
Credit Cards: Visa, Access/Master
No restaurant, but reservations made locally
No Licence (bring your own)
No Wheelchair Access
Children — 30% off, all equipment available
Vegetarian breakfast always available
Pets accommodated in outside stables
Private Car Park
Maddybenny Riding Centre is signposted off the A29 between Portrush and Coleraine.

Hotel
BEECH HILL COUNTRY HOUSE HOTEL
32 Ardmore Road, Derry, Co Londonderry BT47 3QP Tel: (0504) 49279
Fax: 45366
Seamus Donnelly and Helen McDaid

The lure of good food may be the first reason why you turn up at Beech
Hill, for Noel McMeel and his kitchen team produce some stunningly
creative and delicious concoctions; indeed, it is likely that lunch and
dinner here are the best you will find in any hotel anywhere in the
country, and there is no better place to enjoy this dazzling food than
in the sweetly serene and romantic dining room.

But, aside from what is on the plate, the Beech Hill offers a personal
and personality-led welcome, and it boasts all the attenuated concern
of a true family-run place. For those who are breaking with modern
mores and planning getting married, it is noteworthy that Beech
Hill House offers its own chapel — one of the rooms in the house is
blessed — and an ambience of sepulchral sympathy in which to hold
a reception.

Somehow, Beech Hill feels the way hotels used to feel decades ago,
before they fell victim to bland facelessness. As the antithesis of and
an antidote to that modern miasma, Beech Hill stands proud.

Open all year except Xmas day
14 rooms, all en suite
Average Price: standard single £35-£50, standard double £55-£75, suites £10
supplement
No Extra Charges
Credit Cards: Visa, Access/Master, Amex, Diners
Restaurant open 7 days for lunch £11.50, dinner from 6pm £17.95
Full Licence
Wheelchair Access (disabled toilet)
Children welcome
Vegetarian dishes always available
No pets
Enclosed car park
Beech Hill is signposted from the A2 just before you approach Derry city.

Country House
BLACKHEATH HOUSE
112 Killeague Rd, Blackhill, Coleraine, Co Londonderry Tel: (0265) 868433
Joe & Margaret Erwin

Macduff's is the cellar restaurant of Blackheath House, a handsome, quietly unimposing Georgian rectory. Margaret Erwin's cooking is friendly and accessible, with the benefit of almost two decades of experience behind it. The house has six comfortably thoughtful rooms for those who are touring or who wish simply to make a proper night of it.

Thoughtful touches like fresh flowers and fruit in the rooms, acres of bathroom space, a cosy lounge for residents, make the promise of dinner just the cherry on the cake of a valuable place to stay and eat.

Open all year except Xmas
5 rooms, all en suite
Average Price: £30 per person
No Extra Charges
Credit Cards: Visa, Access
Restaurant open for dinner, 7.30pm-9.30pm Tue-Sat (7 days Jul & Aug), from £19
Full Licence
No Wheelchair Access
Not suitable for young children
Vegetarian meals available (give notice please)
No pets
Enclosed car park
Guest sitting room available
Off the A29, seven miles south of Coleraine, four miles north of Garvagh.

Country House
DRENAGH
Limavaddy, Co Londonderry Tel: (05047) 22649
Maj Gen & Mrs P.M. Welch

Drenagh is one of the most highly and most affectionately regarded country houses in the north. People who have stayed here and eaten here are liable to become veritably rhapsodic when discussing its delights.

These ear-bending confessions rhapsodise not just the house itself, though it is a most imposing and serene mansion house dating from 1835, or indeed even the splendid food and the seriousness with which the cuisine is regarded.

No, what zings the strings of people's hearts is the sense of appropriateness which the house engenders, the Welchs' manner of doing things just right. Many of the country houses in Ireland enjoyed such a rash of prosperity and busyness during the fulsome 1980s that they have adapted less well to the more critical and competitive 1990s. Drenagh is a somewhere that demonstrates the charms of the country house vocation and the country vacation, and shows why it is valuable, and fun.

Open Mar-Nov (off season by arrangement)
5 rooms, all en suite or with private bath
Average Price: £40-£50, single supplement £5
No Extra Charges
Credit Cards: Visa, Access/Master
Dinner for guests, book by noon, £25
Wine Licence
No Wheelchair Access
Children — welcome
Vegetarian meals available (please give notice when booking)
No pets
Enclosed car park
On the Limavaddy/Coleraine road, 1 mile out on the left. Go in via the first gate lodge. There is no sign.

Guesthouse

GRANGE LODGE
Grange Rd, Dungannon, Co Tyrone Tel: (08687) 84212
Norah Brown

'It's just instinct', Norah Brown will say about her cooking, 'for I have no training. The dishes are just dishes I like to cook'. Mrs Brown is far too modest. What is especially enjoyable about her cooking in Grange Lodge Country House is the fact that it has the well-won confidence of the domestic cook, so the dishes have the comfort of simple tastes and simple presentation. The pleasure of sitting down in the small dining room in Grange and eating dinner — chicken terrine baked in the Aga, fisherman's moneybag, where fresh salmon is cooked in a filo parcel — gives joy to both body and soul. This food seems ageless, coming as it does out of the inquisitive nature of a confident cook like Mrs Brown, and coming as it does out of a tradition of accomplished domestic cooking, where skills and secrets were handed down in a family from mother to daughter, skills that gave cooks easy-handed confidence and the ability to compile and unravel tastes and flavours in a meal.

So, in Grange, dinner wears an easy rhythm, the surprise of some lemony mushrooms flavoured with garlic and bacon giving way to the succulence of a lamb fricassee with a lemon and thyme sauce, before a sticky pudding of sharp lemon roulade ends a meal in quiet triumph, and you are restored, restored to beaming best.

And what do your thoughts turn to the instant dinner is over? To breakfast, no less, and a bowl of porridge that may have already begun its long overnight simmer in the oven. In the morning, it will receive the expert ministrations of Ralph Brown as he first scatters crystals of brown sugar on top, then annotates the soft grains with a generous splash of Bushmills whiskey before a cloak of rich cream melds with the sugar and the hooch. From first mouthful, you are in culinary heaven, the pleasure points in your body reaching some sort of frothy ferment, a ferment maintained by a generous and expert Ulster Fry.

Open all year except Xmas and New Year
4 rooms, 3 en suite, 1 single with separate bathroom
Average Price: £28 per person sharing, £35 single
No Extra Charges
Credit Cards: Visa, Access/Master
Dinner for guests, £18, book by noon
No Licence (bring your own)
No Wheelchair Access
Children — no children under 12 (no reduction)
Vegetarian meals with prior notice
No pets in house
Enclosed Car Park
1 mile from M1 junction 15. Take A20 to Armagh, then follow signs to Grange.

Points of Entry

These suggested places to stay and places to eat are chosen on account of their proximity to ferries and airports and, of course, their comfort, suitability, their charm.

PORTS

DUN LAOGHAIRE AND DUBLIN NORTH WALL PORTS

Accommodation

ANGLESEA TOWN HOUSE
63 Anglesea Road, Ballsbridge, Dublin 4 Tel: 01-668 3877.
Great big breakfasts are one of the favoured features in Sean and Helen Kirrane's comfortable house, convenient for both the North Wall and the Dun Laoghaire ferries.

AVONDALE HOUSE
Scribblestown, Castleknock, Co Dublin Tel: 01-838 6545.
Very close to both the North Wall ferry and Dublin airport, Frank and Josie Carroll's house is small, great fun.

CHESTNUT LODGE
2 Vesey Place, Monkstown, Co Dublin Tel: 01-280 7860.
Nancy Malone's charming house, and her own charm, make Chestnut one of the nicest places to arrive at, and one of the hardest to leave from.

Restaurants

ELEPHANT & CASTLE
18 Temple Bar, Dublin 2 Tel: 01-679 3121.
The 'no-reservations' policy means one may have to wait for a table, but the E&C's zappy food is perfect for shaking off travel tiredness.

ROLY'S BISTRO
7 Ballsbridge Terrace, Dublin 4 Tel: 01-668 2611.
Romantic, good value, but booking beforehand is usually necessary.

ODELL'S
49 Sandycove Road, Dun Laoghaire Tel: 01-284 2188.
Convenient to the Dun Laoghaire ferry, the food in Odell's is simple, tasty.

ROSSLARE FERRY

Accommodation

FURZIESTOWN HOUSE
Tacumshane, Co Wexford Tel: 053-31376.
For many travellers, Yvonne Pim's house is now a musn't-
miss for first and last nights in Ireland. Delicious cooking.

McMENAMIN'S TOWNHOUSE
2 Auburn Terrace, Wexford, Co Wexford Tel: (053) 46442.
Thoughtful, comfortable, professionally run townhouse.

NEWBAY HOUSE
Newbay, Co Wexford Tel: 053-42779.
Paul and Min Drumm's big pile is one of the friendliest of
the country houses.

Restaurant

EUGENE'S RESTAURANT
Ballyedmond, Co Wexford Tel: (054) 89288.
A pub, a chipper and a restaurant all run by Eugene &
Elizabeth Callaghan. Eugene is a former Roux Brothers'
Young Chef of the year, so expect dazzling food, dazzling
pub food and even dazzling fish and chips.

CORK PORT

Accommodation

GARNISH HOUSE
Western Road, Cork City Tel: 021-275111.
A model B&B amidst the droves of faceless houses on the
Western Road, with Hansi Lucey laying on the charm by
the ton.

SEVEN NORTH MALL
7 North Mall, Cork City Tel: 021-397191.
A beautiful town house with great views over the river and
Angela Hegarty's house also offers excellent value and
super breakfasts.

Restaurant and Accommodation

ISAAC'S HOSTEL
48 MacCurtain Street, Cork City, Hostel Tel: 021-500011.
Restaurant Tel: 021-503805. The food in the Brasserie at

front is very pleasing, strong on flavour. The bathrooms in
the hostel are clean and clever, the rooms smart, the sheets
good, breakfast is fine. Isaac's is closer in style to a pensione
than a hostel.

LARNE AND BELFAST PORTS

Accommodation

ASH ROWAN
12 Windsor Avenue, Belfast BT9 6EE Tel: 0232-661758.
Sam and Evelyn Hazlett's house is quiet and comfortable,
in a quiet and comfortable part of town.

OAKHILL COUNTRY HOUSE
59 Dunmurray Lane, Belfast Tel: (0232) 610658.
May Noble's house is one of the best-regarded places to
stay in the city.

Restaurant

NICK'S WAREHOUSE
35/39 Hill Street, Belfast BT1 Tel: 0232-439690.
Friendly, fun, super food and ambience in Nick and Kathy
Price's inimitable restaurant and winebar.

AIRPORTS

These suggestions give some ideas for places to eat and places to stay if
arriving at one of the local airports in Ireland. If arriving at either Dublin or
Belfast airports, then check the entries for those cities in the Ports section.

SLIGO

Accommodation and Restaurant

GLEBE HOUSE
Coolaney Road, Collooney, Co Sligo Tel: 071-67787.
The bedrooms are simple and straightforward, but Brid
Torrades' cooking in the restaurant is an indulgent delight.

Restaurant

TRUFFLES
11 The Mall, Sligo, Co Sligo Tel: 071-44226.
The greatest pizzas to be found anywhere in the country,
and a great buzzy atmosphere.

KERRY, FARRANFORE AIRPORT

Accommodation and Restaurants, Dingle

DOYLE'S TOWNHOUSE
John Street, Dingle, Co Kerry Tel: 066-51174.
Super rooms in this professional organisation.

BEGINISH RESTAURANT
Green Street, Dingle, Co Kerry Tel: 066-51588.
Splendid cooking in John and Pat Moore's relaxing restaurant.

Accommodation and Restaurants, Kenmare

HAWTHORN HOUSE
Shelbourne Street, Kenmare, Co Kerry Tel: (064) 41035.
A lovely B&B, simple as that.

PACKIE'S RESTAURANT
Henry Street, Kenmare, Co Kerry Tel: 064-41508.
Maura Foley is one of the most celebrated cooks in Ireland, someone who simply does everything right.

WATERFORD

Accommodation and Restaurant

AHERNE'S SEAFOOD BAR AND ACCOMMODATION
163 North Main Street, Youghal, Co Cork Tel: 024-92424.
Great big, comfortable rooms and one of the best fish restaurants in the country

KNOCK

Restaurant and Accommodation

ECHOES RESTAURANT
Main Street, Cong, Co Mayo Tel: 092-46059.
The place to eat when in Mayo: soulful, sublime food from Siobhan Ryan.

TEMPLE HOUSE
Ballymote, Co Sligo Tel: 071-83329.
Many people's favourite country house, not too far north of the airport.

GALWAY

Restaurant

DRIMCONG HOUSE
Moycullen, Co Galway Tel: 091-85515.
Famed country-wide for chef/proprietor Gerry Galvin's culinary cop-on and gastronomic imagination.

Accommodation

MOYCULLEN HOUSE
Moycullen, Co Galway Tel: 091-85566.
Relaxing, laid-back Arts & Crafts house.

NORMAN VILLA
86 Lwr Salthill, Galway Tel: 091-21131.
A small but perfectly beautiful B&B: an aesthete's delight.

SHANNON

Accommodation

BALLYTEIGUE HOUSE
Bruree, nr Charleville, Co Limerick Tel: 063-90575.
Margaret Johnson's house is a great place to wind down after an Atlantic hop.

FERGUS VIEW
Kilnaboy, Corofin, Co Clare Tel: 065-27606.
Lovely cooking from Mary Kelleher in a cosy farmhouse B&B near to Mullaghmore.

Index

142

OTHER TITLES FROM ESTRAGON PRESS

The Bridgestone Irish Food Guide

André Simon Special Award-winning Bridgestone Irish Food Guide is the most comprehensive, independent, critical guide to the very best food in Ireland. From the most committed and creative artisan food producers north and south to the finest restaurants east and west, the Bridgestone Irish Food Guide explores and describes in extensive detail Ireland's inspiring, blossoming food culture. Price: £11.99

The Bridgestone 100 Best Restaurants in Ireland 1994

Evocatively describes the passion, perfectionism and professionalism which fuels Ireland's finest chefs, and gives all the essential information you need to explore the thrilling culinary renaissance blossoming in Ireland's restaurants.
Price: £5.99

The Bridgestone 100 Best Places to Eat in Dublin

The definitive critical independent guide to the finest meals in Dublin, from pizzerias to the grandest restaurants. Simply the essential guide to the capital city's best food. Price: £5.99

The Bridgestone Vegetarian's Guide to Ireland

A comprehensive guide for vegetarians to the finest Irish vegetarian food, written in the style of the award-winning Bridgestone Irish Food Guide. Covering every possible food source, from farms and shops through to restaurants and the best accommodation, this is the definitive guide for vegetarians. Price: £6.99

All titles in the Bridgestone Series from Estragon Press are available in good book stores nationwide.

If you missed any of the Series or have trouble getting them locally, they can be ordered by post direct from the publisher.

Simply fill out the coupon below, enclosing a cheque or money order for the correct amount (add £1.50 per book for postage and packing), and the relevant title(s) will be dispatched to you immediately. Be sure to fill out your address completely, and to print carefully.

Please send me the following title(s) from the Bridgestone series (please tick):

☐ **The Bridgestone Irish Food Guide £11.99**

☐ **The Bridgestone Vegetarian's Guide to Ireland £6.99**

☐ **The Bridgestone 100 Best Places to Eat in Dublin £5.99**

☐ **The Bridgestone 100 Best Restaurants in Ireland £5.99**

☐ **The Bridgestone 100 Best Places to Stay in Ireland £5.99**

I enclose a cheque/money order (delete) for £_____ (including P&P)

....

Name...

Address ....

....

....

....

SEND TO: Estragon Press, Durrus, Co Cork, Ireland